For years Roger McKenzie has
brilliant thought partner when it co
liberation. His thoughtful analysis i
and appreciation for the challenges
around the globe are what is neede

— *Dr Toni Lewis, founder men*

Roger McKenzie's research and writing are putting modern
Pan-African Marxism on a solid theoretical footing, following
— and developing - a trail that was blazed by the likes of Walter
Rodney, Claudia Jones, Amilcar Cabral, Kwame Nkrumah and
W.E.B. Du Bois.

Marx famously said that "the philosophers have only interpreted
the world; the point, however, is to change it." Roger is no ivory
tower theoretician, and his intellectual output is closely linked to
real-world social movements for socialism, for liberation, and against
imperialism, racism, war and ecocide. As such, he joins a global
renaissance of Pan-African thought and activism, grounded in
historical materialism and the struggle for a better world, epitomised
in Africa itself by the new wave of resistant states in the Sahel,
and in the West by groups such as the Black Alliance for Peace.

— *Carlos Martinez, author of 'The East is still Red: Chinese Socialism in the*
21st Century by Praxis Press and co-editor of Friends of Socialist China'

Roger's deep knowledge and commitment to Africa and a
lifetime of anti Racism and trade union solidarity makes him well
placed to write this historical and future analysis.

— *Jeremy Corbyn MP for Islington North*

Roger McKenzie powerfully reminds us that Africa
and its people are not just central to our past but essential to our
collective future. This timely work challenges us to confront the
legacies of colonialism, inequality, and division, and calls for a new
multilateralism rooted in justice, solidarity, and self-determination.
McKenzie's vision is clear: a reborn Africa will be the heart of a
fairer, freer world. A must-read for all who believe in true
global liberation.

— *Bell Ribeiro-Addy MP for Clapham and Brixton Hill and chair of the All*
Party Parliamentary Group on Afrikan Reparations

**"The Rebirth of the African Phoenix
A View from Babylon"
Roger McKenzie**

First Published in 2025 by Manifesto Press

© Roger McKenzie
All rights reserved

MANIFESTO PRESS CO-OPERATIVE LIMITED

Manifesto Press
Ruskin House
23 Coombe Road
Croydon CR1 BD

Typeset in *Futura pt* and *Baskerville*
Designed by Corata Group
Edited by Marine Picard

ISBN 978-1-907464-79-9

chair@manifestopress.coop
manifestopress.coop

manifesto

THE REBIRTH OF THE AFRICAN PHOENIX
A VIEW FROM BABYLON

by Roger McKenzie

To my ancestors with deepest respect. Asante.

CONTENTS

FOREWORD
BY MOLLY DHLAMINI

THE BOOK YOU ARE HOLDING in your hand is aptly titled. If truth be told, it is not a book but an antidote meant to reawaken the sleeping giant — Africa. Like the phoenix, which rises from its ashes, so will our beautiful continent. This is not a wish but an inevitable reality. This prediction surely earns McKenzie the title of a prophet to those who will imbibe in this newfound oasis. His prophecy is clearly coming to pass no matter what. Most of all, it is replete with the same revolutionary messages and prophecies that other African seers and revolutionaries, such as, Bob Marley, Queen Nanny, Yaa Asantewaa, Queen Nzinga, Miriam Makeba, Amilcar Cabral, Malcolm X and Shaka Zulu kaSenzangakhona to count a handful, foretold.

Through the painful account of what people of African descent endured in every part of planet Earth, the book carries the contagious optimism that permeates every chapter. Through the carefully crafted narration, McKenzie takes us back to the screams and shouts of women and men who dreaded the voyage of the infamous Middle Passage. As slaves, those who would not make it, either for ill health or whatever reason, would be thrown to the sea and fed to the sharks. This conjured tragic cases of burial without rituals. The souls of our ancestors hover in the Atlantic Ocean to this day, still cry out for proper burials.

This book could not have come out at an auspicious time. The world superpowers are once again at it preparing and consolidating the new feast, the new scramble of Africa like they did during the Berlin conference in the late 1884, and this is what McKenzie endeavours to illustrate through this book. The form and shape may be different but the essence remains the same. In the book, McKenzie clearly portrays the insidious neo-colonial project that manifests itself through the extraction of the continent's mineral and natural resources by the multinational corporations. It is an open secret that the minerals for green energy that the West most covets are largely in the African continent, which makes the new scramble for Africa imminent.

With a dedicated section on debt, McKenzie illustrates through several examples on how countries in the Caribbean, like Jamaica and many in Africa, can never come out of the vicious cycle of the debt burden. This owes to the manner in which imperialism, the capitalist system and the colonial project were designed for the sustained subjugation of the oppressed.

The book reflects on the campaign that captured the attention of most activists in the late 1990s, which called for the cancellation of the Third World debt. The Jubilee 2000 campaign specifically advocated for the cancellation of odious debt. This issue was particularly resonant for us South Africans. The debt incurred by the racist apartheid regime through loans from German and Swiss banks had to be repaid by the new black government after 1994, which did so faithfully until the debt was fully settled.

McKenzie revives the call for this campaign. He reminds us of the millions of dollars Haiti was forced to repay to its former coloniser, France, after gaining independence. This evokes the sad memories of Mali's struggle during its own independence, when the colonisers retaliated against their decision to sever ties with the metropolis. We are told they even went so far as to destroy school desks to discourage other nations in the region from following Mali's example.

It is no surprise that today, more than ten countries in West and Central Africa are compelled to keep their foreign monetary reserves in the French Treasury, with the currency, the franc CFA, printed in the metropolis. This arrangement generates interest for the French Treasury, while these countries must beg for access to their own funds and at best this is infamously described as 'monetary servitude' in this day and age. This has been an arrangement since 1945. The Mali situation as explained earlier is a stark reminder of how slave masters historically treated rebellious slaves, often maiming or killing them as a warning to others.

However, as McKenzie illustrates throughout the book, no amount of punishment has ever deterred slaves from rebelling or seeking freedom. He shares numerous accounts of these acts of rebellion and highlights the long-lasting spirit of resistance.

The book exposes the hypocrisy of reforms that serve as compensation but fail to adequately address the fundamental injustices of the slave trade. McKenzie argues that slave owners were compensated for their losses when the slave trade was abolished in the mid-1800s, as they were insured, while the enslaved individuals received no compensation. The author further contends that reparations are not only justified but also quantifiable. He refutes the notion that such claims are far-fetched and impossible to achieve. He also advocates for the critical spiritual and cultural dimensions of reparations, which endorse the return of stolen artefacts currently housed in various European museums. Moreover, McKenzie highlights the need to return the skulls of those who were beheaded, drawing parallels to the repatriation of Sara Baartman's remains to South Africa.

The question of reparations serves as a reminder of how those who benefited from apartheid continue to profit from its legacy. This book also reflects on the structural adjustment programs imposed by Bretton Woods institutions, which compelled countries in the Global South to cut social spending in order to service odious debts. This vicious cycle persists today. Recently, a study commissioned by the African Union and conducted by a former President of South Africa investigated illicit financial flows from Africa. McKenzie underscores the significant losses incurred through these illicit flows, which could have been utilised for development. In South Africa, we are acutely aware of the illicit flows of minerals and transfer pricing in the mining industry, which deprive the country of tax revenue and mining communities of the royalties due to them.

This potent book does not lead us to despondency. Rather, it re-energises Africans on the continent and in the diaspora, as well as anyone who identifies with this struggle, to take action and participate in the noble cause of Africa's rebirth. This rebirth is premised on overcoming the condemnation and perpetual subjugation of Africans by the Metropolis and the West. The author illustrates how this subjugation has manifested in various forms — the core issue being the physical, psychological, cultural, social, and spiritual exploitation of Africans, coupled with the looting of their natural and mineral resources.

McKenzie mobilises us to confront the historical damage inflicted on the Democratic Republic of Congo by King Leopold II of Belgium, who claimed the entire country as his personal property. He highlights how the quest for independence in Africa was sabotaged from the very beginning. This, according to McKenzie, is not only through the assassination of Patrice Lumumba and other promising leaders but also by ensuring that post-independence African leaders became mere crisis managers in nations where the political economy remained under the control of the Metropolis, with the ruling class maintaining a firm grip on power.

McKenzie draws a connection between the military-industrial complex, the industrialisation of the West, and the conflicts plaguing the African continent. He underscores the plight of Congo, which has not experienced sustainable peace since its independence due to its abundant resources. The book references certain Western and Gulf states that continue to serve as markets for the illicit minerals fuelling African conflicts.

A crucial point that McKenzie makes is that peace on the continent can contribute towards Africa's development. He reminds us of the Inga project, which has the potential to electrify all of Sub-Saharan Africa and beyond. However, this endeavour would need to follow the model of Ethiopia's Renaissance Dam, where citizens directly funded the project. He correctly contends that international development institutions are often reluctant to finance initiatives that could accelerate Africa's development and industrialisation. Such projects also require the political will of African governments.

For Africans on the continent, this book offers comfort in knowing that our brothers and sisters in the diaspora have not forgotten us, and we have not forgotten them. Together, we can forge ahead to liberate Mother Africa from the shackles of the orchestrated underdevelopment, exploitation, and oppression. McKenzie accurately points out in this book that socialism and Pan-Africanism serve as essential theoretical guides for this rebirth of the mother continent.

May this book not only reignite and reenergise you as you read but also inspire a spirit of contagious optimism that Africa will, against all odds, rise from the ashes like a phoenix.

Molly Dhlamini is an international relations, peace and security practitioner and also serves as a member of the Central Committee of the South African Communist Party.

PUBLISHERS FOREWORD

THE MOST COMPELLING visual image in Roger McKenzie's conjures up in his new book *The African Phoenix* is the map projection which shows Africa in true proportion to other parts of the world.

I had a practical lesson in the urgent need for non-Africans to acquaint themselves with the real size of the continent when, on a mission in still apartheid — ruled Namibia I embarked on a journey up country anticipating with all the confidence of a well-travelled veteran of the cultural centre of metropolitan Europe that I could manage the drive in a day at most.

Eventually, exhausted I arrived to understand that Africa is a very big place and that European perspectives do not suffice.

The great strength of this book is the spirit of uncompromising optimism which takes the fact that the overwhelming number of people on the planet live neither within the borders nor under the formal control of former colonial rulers and that this new dispensation, although contested from within the metropolis, is opening up new possibilities that the rise of China, the growth of the BRICS and the new trade and cooperation synergies create for an Africa awakened.

This is a proudly subjective piece of writing in which Roger McKenzie relates his own political and cultural development to a discovery of an identity rooted in the odyssey of his African ancestors and his own awakening as a subject of the crown in the centre of a system of colonial rule fallen into confusion.

There is his physical encounter with present-day Africa in a visit to Ghana, a cultural shock when confronted with the complexities and tragedies of the slave era, and an examination of the relationship Africans from all parts of the continent have with the land.

He enquires into the legacy of exploitation and the contemporary significance of the dependencies that remain after direct colonialism ended.

The climate emergency figures strongly in his thinking about Africa's future and with it the urgency attached to the conservation of its natural resources, with water not the least important.

As befits a veteran trade union figure he looks deeply at the needs for strong and independent trade unions.

Throughout the book there is a strong strain of anti-imperialist criticism that references the many crimes of the declining colonial powers and the new US imperium.

His intensely subjective standpoint: 'As an African descendant, I am not writing this book with any pretence of detachment. I am looking in and outwards whilst trying to make sense of what is happening. I claim no other expertise than my heritage and a desire to help bring about the revolutionary change that I believe will be necessary to free African peoples on the continent and across the diaspora' stands as a paean of praise for a Pan-Africanism of the 21st century that encompasses not just Africans where they live and work in the continent but the many millions who have an ancestral claim to African identity.

And here McKenzie finds echoes of an anti-imperialist understanding that finds an expression in the most diverse settings.

He argues: 'Rastafarians use the term Babylon to describe corrupt capitalist governments and institutions as well as the colonial world. This seems to me to perfectly describe the current hegemony that runs the world.'

This he contrasts to patterns of traditional land use in which all was held in common and a collective morality rested on the values that arose in such a setting.

The book tackles critical questions for the working-class movement and progressives in the developed capitalist countries that go beyond expressions of sympathy or even acts of charitable giving. Not the least of these is the question of the debt burden that Africa carries that arises from the compromises forced upon nominally independent countries by the global systems operated by the World Bank and the IMF.

The historical and contemporary resonances of the slave trade are strikingly evoked by an intensely personal description of the sites in which captive slaves were held prior to their transport.

The book ranges far and wide across the historical and contemporary problems which face Africa and charts the creative responses of its people to the travails they have suffered over past centuries.

This is a book that makes the connections that lead us to a deeper understanding of the ways in which colonialism mutilated a great continent and a recognition that in its awakening Africa has the capacity to change its own future.

Nick Wright, Chair Manifesto Press Co-operative Limited.

INTRODUCTION

'An overall view of ancient African civilisation and ancient African cultures is required to expunge the myths about the African past, which linger in the mind of Black people everywhere. This is the main revolutionary function of African History.'

— *Walter Rodney*

AFRICA IS A PHOENIX rising from the ashes of the burnt-out colonial world.

Africa, like the phoenix, is an immortal entity that is able to regenerate itself from the ashes of its previous existence.

As in a scene from one of the early Harry Potter movies where the phoenix dies in a blaze of flames before coming back to life stronger than ever, so too will Africa.

For too long there has been a false notion that Africa is a backwater with no discerning or worthwhile history. Nothing could be further from the truth.

Africa is not a country. It is a vast continent of enormous wealth that must always be considered in its full diversity.

It has been the home of great civilisations that were brutally overcome and colonised by a small rump of the planet's population who possessed the military hardware and know-how to subjugate and enslave Africans.

The fact is that the overwhelming number of people on the planet live neither within the borders nor under the formal control of the former colonial rulers. But they have been nevertheless dominated by them for most of the last 500 years.

The good news is that we are now at a major geopolitical tipping point and Africa is at the heart of the construction of a new multilateral world order.

There are no demands for change — as if permission was required. Africans are simply going about the business of constructing a new way of doing things that breaks away from the rules set by the global minority. No part of Africa is asking to leave the plantation. They, and those of us linked to the continent by blood, are doing what our ancestors taught us — leave, fight back and build something new.

This minority, once led by Britain, Spain, Portugal and France — and now themselves overtaken and largely colonised by the United States — are now facing a challenge it has never before experienced.

New global alliances, such as the Brics bloc and the Group of 77 plus China know that the prospects for successfully navigating what will inevitably be a dangerous route out of colonial subjugation depend heavily on Africa.

Trade and the development of new win-win relationships will be at the heart of the arduous road ahead for Africa. It will be a dangerous journey because there has never been a time when people in power have simply stepped aside and ended their exploitation out of the goodness of their hearts. They must be left with no alternative.

The new alliances, such as Brics, explicitly counter the small number of powerful warlike nations that have cast themselves as 'masters of the universe.' They treat Africa and the rest of the global majority as 'unpeople' — like something they have just scraped off the bottom of their shoes.

These wannabe political geniuses regard Africa, in a mixture of arrogance and racism, as mere collateral damage in their quest to boost the profits of the already unimaginably wealthy puppet masters. These largely faceless oligarchs who control how high, when and where politicians jump, are not used to being challenged so will demand swift and brutal action against anyone daring to question their authority.

The financial arms of the global minority, the largely European-directed World Bank and the always US-led International Monetary Fund, have directed the domestic policies of large sections of the African continent since they were created.

At Bretton Woods in 1944 both bodies decided to 'christen' the US dollar as the planet's reserve currency.

It was Christendom once again exerting what it regards as its 'God-given' superiority over a heavily non-Christian Africa.

The new multilateral arrangements being created are a direct challenge to this hegemonic rule.

It is a challenge to the belief of these masters of the universe that everything and anything is up for sale — including whole governments and top judiciaries — such as the US Supreme Court.

The brilliant Arundhati Roy points out that one of the major problems we face is that 'the language of dissent has been co-opted.'

The WTO and World Bank continually publish reports in a way that portrays these predatory organisations as being politically concerned about the plight of people they have systematically exploited for decades.

Outside of activist circles they have been largely successful in painting themselves in a way that masks their primary role of safeguarding the interests of US and European capital.

This moment is a genuine challenge to the power system that has dominated since World War II and the African continent will be at its heart.

This book sets out a series of challenges that must be faced by Africans if this new place for Africa in the new multilateral world is to be achieved.

As the great writer and activist James Baldwin once said: 'Not everything that can be faced can be changed but nothing can be changed until it is faced.'

I begin this book by looking back at my first physical encounter with Africa — a *Homecoming* — when I visited Ghana in the early 1990s.

There will be eight subsequent chapters.

Chapter two, *Money*, will look at the crippling debt burden of African nations and will make the case for a payment strike. This chapter argues for reparations to be paid to Africans across the globe for the evils committed during the transatlantic slave trade and under colonialism.

It also questions whether it is actually possible to repair the damage caused to Africans over 600 years of humiliation and exploitation.

Chapter three examines the important relationship that Africans have to the *Land* after the disruption of the relationship by enslavement and colonialism.

Chapter four, called *Bread*, will look at how such an abundant continent is now forced to import most of its sustenance from abroad and, at times, reduced to begging for emergency food rations when famine hits.

Chapter five discusses the climate emergency that is hitting the continent hard.

Called *Water*, this chapter will look at how the compound, which every human being needs for survival, will be a flashpoint between African nations as resources become more scarce.

Chapter six examines the world of *Work* on the African continent. How can progress be made in building a strong, independent and effective trade union movement on a continent where many people are forced to survive in the informal economy?

This chapter includes a discussion of migration as a key factor in any discussions around work.

Chapter seven concentrates on the role played by Western powers in causing and supporting the efforts for *Peace* across Africa. In particular the way the military-industrial complex continues to make huge profits out of African misery.

This chapter uses the Suez crisis, the Congo and Libya and the current conflict in Sudan to point the finger at the continuing damage caused by Western powers through their interference in African affairs.

Chapter eight will look at the role that *Culture* will play in the 21st-century African renaissance.

Chapter nine makes the connection between the continent and the *Diaspora*. If we believe in creating a new African century then this must include the ancestors of those forcibly removed from the continent during the periods of enslavement to the west and the east.

The final chapter brings together some of my *Reflections* on the key points raised in the book. This includes proposals for a new movement for African unity that celebrates our past, draws strength from our trials and tribulations but recognises that there is a bright future ahead.

Throughout the book I emphasise the resilience of Africans and our permanent state of resistance to racism.

I write this book from the relative comfort of the beast known as Britain. The beast is one of a herd that has tormented Africa for centuries but whose influence is now coming to end — despite its best — or worst — efforts.

As an African descendant, I am not writing this book with any pretence of detachment. I am looking in and outwards whilst trying to make sense of what is happening. I claim no other expertise than my heritage and a desire to help bring about the revolutionary change that I believe will be necessary to free African peoples on the continent and across the diaspora.

This is an optimistic book with the foundational premise that Africans — wherever we are on the globe — must rise up as one people if Africa is to ever rise phoenix-like as a continent to herald in a new world.

What that world will look like does not just depend on the people of Africa and its diaspora. It also relies heavily on the unity of the working-class and peasant communities — Black or white — across the globe.

This book is a view of those challenges from Babylon.

Rastafarians use the term Babylon to describe corrupt capitalist governments and institutions as well as the colonial world. This seems to me to perfectly describe the current hegemony that runs the world.

Our strength to defeat this hegemony comes from our unity. It is a unity that Africans have always fought hard to create in the resistance to exploitation and racism. It will be essential if we are to help deliver the new multilateral world that I believe is a necessity.

Thanks to everyone who has helped me to write this book. All the errors are mine. Only the determination to build a better world is — I hope — shared.

> **'Another world** is not only possible, she is on
> her way. On a quiet day, I can hear her breathing.'
>
> *— Arundhati Roy*

CHAPTER ONE — HOMECOMING

'I am not African because I was born in Africa but because Africa was born in me'

— *Kwame Nkrumah*

'Africa is our centre of gravity, our cultural and spiritual mother and father, our beating heart, no matter where we live on the face of this earth'

— *John Clarke*

TO SAY I WAS NERVOUS about my first homecoming to the African continent in the early 1990s would be an understatement.

Like many English-born people I had been brought up on an unending diet of Africa as a primitive and thoroughly inferior place.

There were not the internet tools available for me to investigate and develop a better knowledge of Africa than the one we were all being fed.

I may have been living in London at this time but it had only been for a short time and, to be honest, my priority was surviving on the relatively meagre wages as a very junior further education lecturer that always meant existing in the capital was going to be a struggle.

But when I got the call at work from the office of the then MP for Tottenham Bernie Grant (much missed) asking me to come and see him and I found out he wanted me to come with him on a delegation to a conference in the Ghanaian capital Accra, I jumped at the chance.

I had flown to Jamaica before as a young child but my memory was that the captains of the flight in both directions were white men. Boarding the flight to Accra and taking a glance to the left was the very first time I had seen an all-Black crew on the flight deck accompanied by an all-Black (women) cabin crew.

I can pretend that I was super cool about this first-time experience but I wasn't. I may have spent most of my life — even by then —

fighting for racial equality and talking about how any black person could do anything any white person could do but the reality of the conditioning that I had been subjected to did — in all honesty — kick in.

Was I really going to be safe in the air in the hands of black people? Was I actually going to make it to Africa — the land of my ancestors?

Of course there were no problems at all and I recall the flight as really comfortable and enjoyable being surrounded by so many Africans.

Looking back I can now reflect on the power of the conditioning that we all go through. If I, with my politics, was forced to think twice then how do others — Black or white — but without the same commitment to equality and, perhaps, the understanding that I claim to have, manage to navigate this situation.

The other thing I remember about the journey was that I did not watch any of the films that were on offer. Instead I was transfixed by the map by which it was possible to follow the journey.

When you follow the map for the 6 to 8 hours that it takes to cross the ancestral burial ground otherwise known as the Atlantic Ocean to reach what is now known as the Americas, you don't get the same sense of distance. All you see on the map is blue for the sea.

New York is slightly further than Accra in miles but travelling the 3,000 miles or so from London to Ghana's capital gives a better feel for the distance and the sheer size of the African continent.

It also makes you realise just how relatively tiny these European kingdoms were that colonised the continent at the point of superior weaponry and a seemingly endless appetite for brutality.

Years later I got hold of the Peter's Projection map that presents countries in their true proportion to one another.

Traditional map projections have tended to show countries incorrectly in proportion to one another, exaggerating the size of high-latitude countries such as Canada and making tropical regions such as Africa appear much smaller than they actually are.

In 1855 clergyman James Gall started the challenge to the map orthodoxy when he unveiled his new version of the world map at the British Association for the Advancement of Science's meeting in Glasgow.

More than 120 years later, German historian Arno Peters announced his variation on Gall's work.

In 1973 Peters presented the 'Peters world map', but it wasn't until 1986 that the name 'Gall-Peters projection' was coined.

The map shook the status quo of the world of cartography with its challenge to the orthodoxy which prioritised the nations of the Global North.

The Gall-Peters map was a revolution in cartography and, of course, was far from welcomed by the ruling class in whose interest it remained to portray the Global South as inferior.

The Gall-Peters map should be seen as an important symbol of the power of how places, things and people are represented.

The map provides a representation of the world that prioritises the accuracy of land masses' areas over their shapes and shows the continents in their relative size, which is often distorted in traditional map projections.

The map challenges the Eurocentric view of the world which diminishes the importance of regions other than Europe and North America.

This new perspective provides a revolutionary break from the Eurocentric view that has dominated maps for centuries — the one taught in schools and which has become part of the framing of the dominance of the Europeans and North Americans.

By representing the regions' land area accurately, it challenges our traditional beliefs and enables us to see the world in a new light.

The reality is that the African continent has a land area of 11.7 million square miles — enough to fit in the US, China, India, Japan, and Mexico, for starters, combined. It is home to around 1.6 billion, equivalent to more than 18 per cent of the world's population.

I was ignorant of any of this during all those geography lessons when my main concern was getting through the ordeal of my classmates sniggering over a primitive continent whose only history apparently involved enslavement or Egypt.

Although Kemet — to give it its real name — was rarely identified as belonging to the African continent.

Kemet was often translated as the 'Black Land'. It is said to refer to the fertile, dark soil along the Nile River, the lifeblood of the ancient lands.

The name Egypt that is used commonly in English and many other languages, derives from the Greek word Aigyptos. The name came into common usage during the Greek classical era and has remained in use ever since.

None of this was ever even remotely touched on throughout my schooling.

Africa has suffered centuries of being diminished as a primitive and unimportant land mass inhabited by brainless black savages that could only prosper with the aid of 'the white man'. This is a key part of the justification of racism that underpins capitalism.

When I learned I was going to Africa I wondered what I would do and how I would feel when I landed. It was, after all, a real homecoming. I had no idea of my ancestry at the time. For all I knew I could have been treading the same ground as my ancestors.

Based on slave ship records, the Akan people — part of the Asante kingdom of West Africa, including Ghana — provided the bulk of people enslaved in Jamaica — where both my parents were born.

As embarrassing as it now sounds, after descending from the plane I remember dropping to my knees, kissing the ground and quietly saying 'I'm home'.

I spent the week or so in Accra learning much about the Pan-African movement from many who had played a pivotal role for decades. I also developed a deeper understanding of the movement for reparations.

But nothing prepared me for the emotions that would engulf me when we visited Elmina Castle.

During the mid-1980s I visited the Buchenwald concentration camp in the former German Democratic Republic. Like many people who visit these death camps, I found the whole experience extremely harrowing.

The first prisoners in Buchenwald were communists followed by other political prisoners, trade unionists, Jews, Poles, Slavs, Soviet prisoners of war, Roma, the mentally ill and physically disabled.

In all 280,000 prisoners passed through the camp, compelled to work as slave labour with around 56,545 deaths.

There may have been black people in the camp — I don't know. But it was difficult to know just how much direct skin I had in the area — not that this really mattered given the scale of the atrocities committed by the Nazis.

There was no doubt in my mind though that Elmina was an entirely different proposition — as harrowing as the experience of Buchenwald was.

I knew that Africans — maybe even some of my ancestors — had been dragged across many miles to this castle ahead of a horrific journey into the unknown.

The castle looks out over the sacred burial ground otherwise known as the Atlantic Ocean.

Many arriving in shackles to the fort would have been from far inland where they were surrounded and captured by the slave catchers as they went about their daily business. Their families often could only guess what had happened to them.

The only certainties were that they would never see their kin again and that they also were being hunted.

Elmina, built in 1482 by the Portuguese to protect their trade in gold, is thought to be the oldest surviving European building in sub-Saharan Africa. It was not built as a slave trading castle — it became that later.

The transition of Elmina Castle from a trading post to becoming the first European slave-trading post reflected the growth of the trade in human beings that was becoming one of the dominant factors in global trade during the 16th and 17th centuries.

As the Portuguese and other European powers began establishing colonies in the Americas, the demand for cheap or free labour dramatically increased.

This was particularly the case as the indigenous populations of the Americas were being wiped out by the ruthless and deadly conquest for gold and other what they considered to be essential materials plus the diseases brought over by the Europeans.

To meet labour shortages and to maximise profits, the European powers turned to Africa to supply the labour, marking the beginning of the brutal enslavement of Africans.

Elmina Castle, with its strategic location and what must have been formidable fortifications, quickly became a significant node in this horrific network.

The castle's dungeons, initially designed for storing trading goods, were 'repurposed' to imprison enslaved Africans before their forced transportation across the Atlantic.

The Portuguese, and later the Dutch and the British, who took control of the castle, exploited the existing local conflicts and rivalries to their advantage.

The Europeans turned Africans against Africans in return for a few baubles that were usually of no real value to them.

Weapons and other goods were provided to local African leaders in return for slaves.

The simple fact is that the transatlantic trade in human beings could likely have never been possible without the exploitation of local rivalries leading to the involvement of Africans assisting in the bondage of other Africans.

It is the same story on the East coast of Africa. The enslavement of Africans for the eastern slave trade is also an important story but less told than the trade across the Atlantic.

The Indian Ocean coast of Africa became a slave trade 'hub' in its own right with the west coast of India.

Known as the 'Oriental' or Eastern slave trade, from the 7th century enslaved Africans were captured and transported to the Middle East, North Africa and India.

It was different to the transatlantic slave trade in that the demand was primarily for domestic servants, and mostly women were captured to supply the trade.

This trade in human beings through the east coast of Africa lasted well into the 19th century only ending when the British ended slavery in India in 1843.

In the eastern slave trade Africans were largely captured from the countries now known as Kenya, Tanzania, Mozambique and the island of Madagascar. They also came from countries now known as Mali, Niger, Chad and Sudan and Horn of Africa nations known as Djibouti, Somalia and Ethiopia.

The enslaved women were often forced to marry their masters, or had children by them and the children were often freed by their fathers.

Over time, the enslaved Africans tended to become part of the local population.

The demand for women slaves in the eastern slave trade meant that the many men who were captured at the same time as the women remained as slaves in Africa.

There were many plantations in, for example, Kenya where the enslaved men were forced to work.

It is estimated that in the 17th century, about 10,000 slaves per year were sold to North Africa and the Middle East.

There was a large domestic slave population in this area and slavery was an accepted form of labour amongst the rulers of the different kingdoms.

Enslaved Africans were sold from the east coast to other areas including the Persian Gulf and India for hundreds of years.

The numbers of enslaved Africans sold to these areas increased in the late 18th century as French merchants bought slaves from East Africa for the growing sugar plantations on the French-owned islands in the Indian Ocean.

Brazilian merchants also began buying slaves from the same area for the sugar plantations in Brazil, after 1800.

Then, trade to the Persian Gulf and India increased rapidly. By the early 19th century about 30,000 people were being sold into slavery from eastern Africa.

They were being bought and sold through the main centre of the trade on the island of Zanzibar (off the east coast of Africa, of what is now the country of Tanzania).

It has been estimated that over the twelve centuries from 750 to the 20th century (slavery continued in this area well into the 20th century, and beyond) almost 12 million enslaved Africans were traded to the Middle East, North Africa and India. This is likely to be a gross underestimate.

The eastern slave trade lasted far longer than the transatlantic slave trade.

But like the trade through castles such as Elmina, it forcibly stripped the continent of vast swathes of the population.

The transformation of Elmina back on the West coast is an important moment in history as it marks a change and expansion of world trade.

Elmina was now a holding place for enslaved Africans before they were subjected to the barbaric journey deep in the bowels of a ship during what became known as the Middle Passage.

Given past television programmes such as the epic Roots and the dominance of the US TV and film industry it is easy to fall for the lie that most Africans were sent for sale to US plantations.

This is far from the truth.

Elmina and the other slave forts sent most enslaved Africans to South America. Brazil was the single largest recipient of enslaved Africans — largely from further south of Ghana in what is now known as Angola.

My ancestors may well have been part of the countless human beings who suffered almost unimaginable indignities at the hands of the slavers. My ancestors may even have been amongst the women that the head of the castle would look down and choose for his sick pleasure each night.

If not Elmina then it would have been one of the other similar torture venues along the West African coast.

As the minibus that carried our party the nearly 100 miles from Accra to Elmina neared the castle I remember feeling a deep knot in my stomach coupled with a chill across my back — despite the soaring temperature.

It is a feeling that I will never forget and returns every time I think about the visit to Elmina Castle — one that has returned as I write these lines.

The feeling grew more intense as we caught sight of the castle for the first time and did not leave me for days afterwards.

The first thing I remember as we left the minibus and approached the whitewashed castle on foot was the overpowering smell of fish and the sight of the fishermen and their nets below as they went about their business.

Looking back I wonder now what the Portuguese who first arrived in 1471 made of the sight of these locals going about their business? They would not have looked like the fishermen and women that we imagine today.

The story goes that the Portuguese encountered villagers adorned in ornate gold jewellery. The historical records suggest that the Portuguese were amazed by the abundance of gold and that even the 'poorest' person in the village was able to dress themselves in the priceless gem.

The name Gold Coast was given to the region for a reason. The place was awash with gold.

To the locals in Elmina, the people they saw arriving to visit the Castle were the latest in a long line of 'wanna-be' Africans.

Those of us from the diaspora who seek African unity should never play down the differences that sometimes exist between Africans on the continent whose families — as far as they know — have never been enslaved towards those who most definitely have been.

I have heard and experienced this difference but not as often as I have been greeted with 'welcome home', as I return to the continent.

At the end of the narrow bridge entering the castle there is a marble plaque that reads:

'In Everlasting Memory of the anguish of our ancestors may those who died rest in peace. May those who return find their roots. May humanity never again perpetrate such injustice against humanity. We the living vow to uphold this.'

After the stark reality rather than the theory of what we were entering had hit me our group entered a whitewashed courtyard. I remember feeling how appropriate the whitewashing was.

Around the edge of this courtyard were the dungeons. They either held all men or all women. The women's dungeon seemed specifically located in the castle so that the soon-to-be transported girls and women could be more easily chosen as 'entertainment' for the guards.

After Bernie Grant persuaded a worker at the castle to be the guide of this unofficial tour we walked around — many of us in tears as we saw and heard about the treatment of the captured Africans who were being prepared for the journey across the ocean.

Things got really emotional for our party when we reached the dungeon known as the Door of No Return.

I remember the infamous dungeon as low and dark with a single slit that allowed a view of a narrow strip of land separating the castle from the sea. This is where small boats would await to force the captive and heavily chained human beings to the larger ships on which they would be shipped like animals for slaughter across the ocean.

The so-called Middle Passage of the transatlantic slave trade was horrific. It's actually hard to find the words that one feels thinking about your ancestors trying to endure these conditions.

Many historians view the Middle Passage as the largest movement of people from one location to another in history, as somewhere around 20 million Africans were forcibly transported from the early 1500s to the latter half of the 19th century.

Conditions on the ships were cruel and disgusting. But nobody should ever believe that the enslaved Africans just accepted their lot.

There are numerous examples of rebellions on board these torture chambers.

In 1742, the Jolly Batchelor was attacked by enslaved Africans while it was at dock in what became known as the Sierra Leone River.

The crew were killed during the fighting and the victorious Africans freed themselves and the people who were being held captive in the hold of the ship.

In 1752, the Bristol-based ship, The Marlborough, was taken over by enslaved Africans while it was sailing across the Atlantic. Many of the crew were killed and those that survived were forced to sail the ship back to Africa from where the enslaved Africans were freed.

One of the most famous rebellions recorded was on board The Amistad in 1839.

The ship was carrying enslaved Africans to a Spanish-owned plantation in Cuba. A group of Africans managed to escape from their chains and took control of the ship, killing several of the crew in the process.

The Africans were eventually re-captured and a court hearing was called to decide their fate. In a landmark ruling, the US Supreme Court granted the enslaved Africans their freedom.

This makes me enormously proud. I have no way of knowing the truth but I like to picture my ancestors being part of any uprisings on the ships they were forced on.

Historians have estimated that something in excess of 2 million Africans died during the Middle Passage.

Many died due to cramped conditions, which allowed diseases like measles and smallpox to quickly spread. Unsanitary conditions led to contaminated drinking water, leading to dysentery, diarrhoea, and dehydration.

Many also arrived at their destination covered in sores and suffering from fever.

Africans were placed below deck, with males and females separated. Men and boys were placed toward the front and women and girls toward the back.

During the voyage across the Middle Passage, Africans were usually fed only once or twice a day. Some refused to eat, as a form of protest against their abduction. If they refused, they were often force-fed by their captors.

But many Africans also chose to throw themselves into the sea when the chance presented itself — favouring death to enslavement.

Sharks are said to have regularly followed slave ships so that they could feast on Africans who were thrown overboard or who chose death.

These deaths are why I refer to the Atlantic Ocean as a sacred burial ground.

The Middle Passage usually took more than seven weeks, with the length of the voyage depending on weather conditions in the Atlantic Ocean.

There were Middle Passage destination ports in all regions of the American Colonies. Sullivan's Island in South Carolina holds the unfortunate distinction of being the port where the highest number of Africans entered the American Colonies.

After arriving in the so-called New World, some Africans escaped from their captors. They formed 'Maroon Colonies' in remote regions of the American Colonies, including South Carolina and Florida.

For those forced onto plantations, life expectancy was around five years. They simply worked the Africans to death and replaced them with a new batch as they died out.

The fact is we were never meant to survive either enslavement or colonialism as individuals. All that was required was that there was a ready supply of us to replace those of us that were used and abused.

Coming home to Africa is no small occurrence. I have now been to the north, south, east and west of the continent — although never to the central regions.

It feels special every time I have visited the continent whether for work or a holiday — but it is always a pleasure — even with the emotions of Elmina.

Part of the rebirth of Africa will be this homecoming, in both a physical and spiritual sense, of Africans across the diaspora.

This will be as painful for many as it will be eye-opening. But it will be a necessary step in reconnecting us with our ancestral home.

Some African nations are now offering a route to citizenship for anyone who can show they are the descendants of enslaved Africans.

A new law allows citizenship to anyone over 18 who does not already hold other African citizenship and can provide proof that an ancestor was deported via the slave trade from anywhere in sub-Saharan Africa.

Beninese authorities accept DNA tests, authenticated testimonies and family records.

The coastal town of Ouidah was one of Africa's most active slave-trading ports in the 18th and 19th centuries.

Benin has openly acknowledged its role in the slave trade, a stance not shared by many other African nations that participated. In the 1990s, Benin hosted an international conference, sponsored by UNESCO, to examine how and where slaves were sold.

And in 1999, President Mathieu Kérékou fell to his knees whilst visiting a church in Baltimore and issued an apology to African Americans for Africa's involvement in the slave trade.

Memorial sites are mostly in Ouidah. Benin has its own 'Door of No Return', which marks the point from which many enslaved people were shipped across the Atlantic, as well as the town's history museum.

Benin is not the first country to grant citizenship to descendants of slaves. Last year Ghana naturalised 524 African Americans after the West African country's president, Nana Akufo-Addo, invited them to 'come home' in 2019.

This marked the 400th anniversary of the arrival of the first enslaved Africans in Virginia in the US during 1619.

Ghana's Tourism Authority and the Office of Diaspora Affairs have extended the program into 'Beyond the Return', which fosters the relationship with diasporans.

Hundreds have been granted citizenship, including people from Britain, Canada and Jamaica.

The path to Ghanaian citizenship is less clearly defined than the route in Benin. The granting of citizenship must come from a concession from Ghana's presidency, a process made legal under the 2000 Citizenship Act.

Citizenship in Ghana is granted to those residing in Ghana who have told the Office of Diaspora Affairs that they are interested in citizenship.

Ghana's government in part describes the programme as a benefit to the economy and focuses on investment opportunities for those wishing to relocate.

I likely will never take up the opportunity of citizenship of any African country — all of which were created by lines drawn by a colonialist on a map. I absolutely understand why others might want to take the opportunity though. It is, after all, a tangible reconnection to Mother Africa — a way of remembering.

In Ouidah there is a 'Tree of Forgetfulness', where enslaved people were said to be symbolically forced to forget their past lives.

We must develop our own methods of remembering. This is why Elmina Castle and other similar places of terror and heartache must be preserved and become as important as the Nazi death camps of Europe.

Remembering on its own will never be enough. Homecoming must be accompanied by action to bring about justice for the sins of the past — which I discuss in the next chapter *Money*.

'Our struggle is also a struggle of memory against forgetting.'

— *South African Freedom Charter*

CHAPTER TWO – MONEY

'**If you owe** the bank $100, that's your problem.
If you owe the bank $100 million, that's the bank's
problem.'

— J Paul Getty

THE PRINCIPLE OF NATIONS making payments for the
damages that they have caused is not a new one. Neither are
the controversies over who should pay and who is entitled to receive
any payments.

Enslaved Africans, their descendants or even the countries from
which these people were taken were certainly not considered worthy
of payment.

Rich European powers stole more than 20 million people out of
Africa, shackled and enslaved them to transport them across the
Atlantic, worked them to the bone and then underdeveloped the
African continent through colonisation. They then expected African
nations to pay them back for the 'privilege' of being exploited.

Any talk of reparations for the evils of slavery and colonialism
is waved away with one dismissive hand while the other one is
stretched out in the expectation that African nations pay back, with
massive interest, the debt they owe.

The Africa Reparations Movement (ARM UK) was set up by the
former MP for Tottenham the late Bernie Grant.

Grant was an uncompromising supporter of reparations — something
his constituency successor David Lammy — Labour's current foreign
secretary — has distanced himself from.

ARM UK was set up after a Conference on Reparations held in
Nigeria in 1993 with the aim of seeking reparations for the harm
done to Africa and the African diaspora through enslavement,
colonisation, and racism.

But it would be wrong to think that reparations is some new idea
that has been dreamt up by Africans with some sort of chip on
their shoulders.

Making reparations for enslavement has a long tradition. In the US the first recorded case of a payment of reparations for enslavement was to a woman called Belinda Royall in 1783.

Royall, who was born in what is now known as Ghana was paid a pension as compensation for her enslavement.

From 1804 Haitians were paying their former colonial rulers France for the privilege of being free from enslavement.

Over the following century Haiti was forced to pay former slaveholders and their descendants the equivalent of around £23 billion.

These included the Empress of Brazil; the son-in-law of the Russian Emperor Nicholas I, Germany's last imperial chancellor; and Gaston de Galliffet, the French general known as the 'butcher of the Commune' for crushing an insurrection in Paris in 1871.

They also contributed towards the profits of Crédit Industriel et Commercial in France — the bank that helped to finance the construction of the Eiffel Tower.

Britain also thought it was best to make reparations payments to slave owners rather than to those who had been enslaved.

The Slavery Abolition Act of 1833 made a mockery of the freeing of enslaved Africans by making around 40,000 payments worth billions in today's money to slave owners.

The largest total amount paid in reparation to a slave owner was made to Sir John Gladstone, the father of Prime Minister William Gladstone.

He was paid the equivalent of more than 10 million in today's money for 'losing his property' of £2,508 enslaved Africans who already enriched him on his nine plantations in the Caribbean.

The families of slave owners remained rich while those of enslaved Africans were often left in the most gut-wrenching poverty imaginable.

These simple reversals of what anyone might reasonably regard as justice are largely either unknown or ignored.

Part of our job must be to place the facts in front of people when they claim that reparations are either impossible or unreasonable.

Reparations for the descendants of enslaved Africans, whatever the form of the payments, are entirely reasonable and long overdue.

As well as the amounts that should be paid the issue that vexes so many people is around who should pay.

If, as I believe, only those who have benefitted from the transatlantic slave trade should be responsible for paying reparations, then the question is who are those with responsibility?

There appears to be no reasonable case for reparations to be paid by workers who themselves faced exploitation.

Instead, the companies and individuals — and their descendants that profited from the 'earnings' of those organisations must bear responsibility for making reparations to the ancestors of enslaved Africans.

One example is Richard Drax, the former Tory MP for South Dorset, who was one of the wealthiest landowners in the House of Commons. He was worth more than £130 million.

Much of his wealth comes from his family's involvement in the enslavement of Africans.

The Drax family used enslaved Africans to cultivate sugar on plantations on the Caribbean islands of Barbados and Jamaica.

Drax remains the owner of the family's 621-acre slave plantation, Drax Hall in Barbados. He is an extreme example where the huge wealth made by members of the British working class can be traced directly back to the transatlantic slave trade.

As I mentioned earlier, members of parliament were not slow to pay themselves large sums in reparations for loss of 'property' as they passed the 1833 act to abolish slavery.

Their ancestors will still be around and should be made to repay.

Lloyd's of London was also a big player in the slave trade.

The insurance of ships, cargo and captured enslaved persons facilitated the growth of the transatlantic slave trade. This means the customers of Lloyd's, as well as members of its governing body, had significant connections to the transatlantic slave trade.

Lloyd's of London, which was founded in 1688, said in 2023 that it was 'deeply sorry' for these links after an independent report found the company had played a 'significant role' in enabling the transatlantic trade.

Lloyd's said it was committed to tackling inequality and would invest £40m in helping impacted communities.

After protests swept across the world in 2020 following the killing of African American George Floyd by the police, pressure mounted on companies to address links to slavery and tackle racial inequality.

At the time, Lloyd's apologised for its historical links to the slave trade and commissioned the independent report.

Alexandre White, one of the professors behind the study, made clear that Lloyd's formed part of 'a sophisticated network of financial interests and activities' which made the transatlantic slave trade possible.

But he said the material offered very little about the people who were 'captured and enslaved under the practices facilitated by the Lloyd's market.'

He said: 'While the activities of insurers in the city of London may seem far removed from the plantations, ships and the violent spaces of imprisonment along the coast of Africa, the financial architectures developed at Lloyd's helped maintain the institution of slavery.'

'The insurance of ships, cargo and captured enslaved persons facilitated the growth of the transatlantic slave trade,' said Mr White, concluding that customers of 'Lloyd's, as well as members of its governing body, had 'significant connections to the transatlantic slave trade.'

Responding to the review, chairman Bruce Carnegie-Brown said: 'We're deeply sorry for this period of our history and the enormous suffering caused to individuals and communities both then and today.'

'We're resolved to take action by addressing the inequalities still seen and experienced by black and ethnically diverse individuals.'

The firm vowed to put in place a 'comprehensive programme of initiatives' to help people from diverse ethnic backgrounds 'participate and progress from the classroom to the boardroom.' There has been no discernable progress in fulfilling this promise.

Kehinde Andrews, Professor of Black Studies at the University of Birmingham, dismissed the move as a 'PR exercise' and 'offensive.'

Professor Andrews said: 'If they were serious they would be proposing a transfer of wealth to the descendants of the enslaved, not a diversity scheme for so-called 'ethnically diverse' people, which any corporation should be doing.'

The comments from Professor Andrews underscore the importance of being clear-eyed about the difference between performative words and actions and things that actually make a material difference to the lives of the descendants of enslaved Africans.

But Lloyd's is clearly a beneficiary of the slave trade and must not be allowed, alongside so many other companies who benefitted, to get away with not paying what is due. Banks are clearly heavily involved in the management of debt and payments across the globe.

The debt that is owed by African countries to world financial institutions and the richer nations is on a scale that is almost imaginable.

But we can get a sense of the control exerted by this debt by looking at our own personal circumstances.

Most of us have to make decisions about whether we can engage in the smallest activity or pay for even the smallest necessity or — if we are lucky — luxury, depending on how much money we have available.

Imagine this for a country in Africa wondering how to balance making sure that the people have food to eat, that they have access to education and healthcare against paying back the debt that they owe.

According to figures from the United Nations public debt on the African continent stands at around 1.5 trillion. This means Africa's public debt has increased by around 183 per cent since 2010, roughly four times higher than its growth rate of Gross Domestic Product (GDP).

Africa's share of external debt, the money it owes other nations or the International Monetary Fund (IMF) or the World Bank, rose from around 19 per cent in 2010 to just shy of 29 per cent in 2022.

External debt as a share of exports, particularly important for Africa where many countries rely heavily on exports, has risen from 74.5 per cent, over the same period, to a staggering 140 per cent.

All of this is disturbing enough but more so when you consider that a debt cancellation agreement for low-income countries was reached in 2005 by the foreign ministers of the group of seven leading industrial nations.

This agreement led to $130 billion dollars (£104 billion) of debt being cancelled for 36 countries.

According to Afreximbank, Africa's debt is primarily external, with the region's external debt reaching US$1.2 trillion (just under £1 trillion) by 2023, making up nearly 60 per cent of its total public debt.

Over the past 15 years, this external debt has more than doubled, increasing from 18.8 per cent of GDP in 2008 to 41.6 per cent in 2023.

Before the pandemic, over 30 African countries were spending more on paying off debt than on healthcare, showing just how much debt is weighing on their budgets.

Also, the fact that most of Africa's debt is concentrated in just a few countries makes the problem even worse.

According to Afreximbank, in 2023, 67 per cent of the continent's external debt was held by just 10 countries: Egypt, South Africa, Nigeria, Morocco, Mozambique, Angola, Kenya, Tunisia, Sudan, and Ghana.

These countries are carrying a much bigger debt load compared to the rest, which makes them more vulnerable when debt payments spike.

A recent report by Global Firepower which tracks external debt as part of its annual defence review, shows that Egypt has the highest external debt in Africa, standing at the equivalent of £83.4 billion, ranking 50th globally.

South Africa follows closely in second place with £47.2 billion, ranked 56th globally. Angola comes in third with £36.8 billion, ranked 65th worldwide.

Whilst the level of a country's debt is worrying enough, arguably even more of a worry is the country's debt relative to its GDP.

When, as in some African nations, debt is proportionate to GDP, the country risks experiencing an economic catastrophe.

The primary drawback of a high external debt-to-GDP ratio is the increased vulnerability it poses to external shocks and fluctuations in global financial markets.

This places African nations even more at the behest of the rich Western nations and the financial institutions.

In times of crisis, such nations may find themselves with no room for manoeuvre and are forced to cut what is left of their public services and to seek bailouts from international institutions such as the World Bank and IMF.

Debt Justice estimates that 'people in 54 countries are currently living in debt crisis, up from 31 in 2018 and 22 in 2015.'

Debt Justice says a debt crisis takes place where debt leads to human rights or life being denied.

I'm not great at maths but even by my calculations, that means that things are getting worse for the people of the Global South rather than better.

On a geopolitical level, debt must be seen as one of the main reasons for the halting of the forward march of the past Third World or Global South project.

The necessary 'unpausing' of the march can only really take place if this issue of the debt owed by Africa and the rest of the Global South is addressed.

We will not see a healthy rebirth of the African Phoenix until this debt question is dealt with.

To press the button to restart the project in a way that will make a difference we have to stop walking the wheel that brings us back to the same place with every step.

Something different has to be done for us to end up in a different place.

We hear a lot about the need for the rich Global North nations to make money available to Africa, its diaspora and the rest of the Global South as reparations for the damage that their carbon emissions have caused to the environment.

I agree. I think they should urgently do this. But often left out of this equation is the fact that the Global North deliberately underdeveloped the South so that they could steal, whether through military power or forced labour, the abundant resources of the African continent.

This theft has institutionalised poverty across Africa. It has forced nations on the continent to have to seek external financial support to support the pretence that they are actually in charge of their economies.

It is merely a pretence that they are not completely beholden to the financial institutions, monopoly capital and the rich Western powers.

The number of people in Africa living in extreme poverty is something in the region of 430 million of its 1.6 billion population.

This might only change by degrees with some performative largesse by the rich Western powers but the reality is the nations of Africa will remain in perpetual debt unless they can break free from what can only be described as a most vicious cycle.

I think if the rich nations and the likes of the World Bank and the IMF refuse to cancel the debt, as they should, then the nations of Africa should take collective action and simply refuse to pay on the basis that they can't afford to pay.

Some parts of Africa are already taking collective action to end the long exploitation of the legacy of colonial exploitation.

In West Africa some nations are rising up against the exploitation of the Global North where the rich in the richest countries continue to get richer whilst the working class and peasant communities in the poorer nations — the darker nations — continue to get poorer.

At first glance this might seem like a far-fetched proposal but it's actually happened before.

Argentina, Ecuador and Paraguay in the past have all refused to repay debts to the World Bank, the IMF and other financial institutions.

When each of these countries stopped paying they all managed to improve wages, pensions and the living conditions of the population.

In an act rarely mentioned, Ecuador even expelled the World Bank's permanent representative to their country.

They also evicted the IMF from its offices within Ecuador's Central Bank and resigned from the International Centre for the Settlement of Investment Disputes, the tribunal of the World Bank, a road that Bolivia had travelled two years earlier.

Those nations returned to economic and financial difficulties when they returned to 'playing the rules' — which seems primarily to be anything that the United States says that it is.

Whilst I have seen plenty of arguments from the rich nations of the world and the financial institutions about why such a move would be irresponsible I have seen none that says they can't do it.

I have also seen no reasons why this 'can't pay — won't pay' approach could not be replicated across Africa or any other part of the Global South and the money used to invest in their own countries to alleviate poverty.

I realise that for this approach to take place the client regimes or gatekeepers installed by the former colonial powers will need to be removed. That's of course a job for the people on the ground to carry out.

There is no incentive for the numerous eye-wateringly rich individuals and families to bite the hand that feeds the hand that keeps them in power without being forced to do so. But as the poor get poorer and the rich get richer something will inevitably give.

Our job as socialists is to make sure that when change comes it is not by another regime bent on bleeding the people dry but one that puts people before profits and colonial domination.

There are opportunities for the rich nations of the Global North to at least negotiate their way out of the debt crisis that has been largely caused by them.

The increasingly discredited United Nations climate conferences have been used by African nations to have the rich Western powers pay some money towards the impact of the climate emergency.

I will explore the impact of the climate emergency in the chapter *Water* but the issue of climate debt is a reversal on who owes who and what do they owe that I wanted to tackle at this point.

The argument about debt is often framed in terms of Africa and other parts of the Global South having to pay back what they allegedly owe to the already rich nations and the financial institutions that they largely control.

Rarely is the debate on debt framed in a way that dares to suggest that the rich nations of the West owe African nations for the rape, pillage and exploitation they have exacted on the continent.

I challenge this view and suggest that reparatory justice can be met in a number of ways.

One of those is to assist in repairing the vast environmental damage that has been caused by the rich nations of the Global North.

I go into this damage in more detail in the chapter called Water.

Here though I want to deal with the financial repayments that would need to be made to contribute towards reparations.

The United Nations Conference of the Parties (COP) process has continually failed to deliver any realistic finance to help developing countries deal with the impact of the worsening climate emergency, as 144 countries face the worst debt crisis in history.

The fact that there are 193 UN-recognised sovereign countries illustrates the depth of the debt crisis facing the beleaguered Global South.

A report earlier this year by the campaign group Debt Relief International for Norwegian Church Aid (DRI) shows that repaying the debt is absorbing 41.5 per cent of budget revenues, 41.6 per cent of spending, and 8.4 per cent of Gross Domestic Product on average across the 144 developing countries.

Health and education budgets have been slashed by debt-enslaved countries in Africa as nearly half of the national budgets are used to pay creditors.

This paralysing debt enslavement halts any attempts by the world's poorest nations to break away from the control of the self-appointed 'masters of the universe' — the small but powerful cabal of Western countries led by the United States.

Africa needs to escape this extractive, exploitative and abusive relationship that it has been subjected to by Western powers.

I was once told that there is little point in merely finding ways to cope with an abusive relationship — one must find the means and the strength to leave it.

It is unacceptable for a continent as rich and abundant as Africa to be in a position where it imports around 85 per cent of its food — with much of this food only affordable to tourists and the well-to-do on the continent.

Dagfinn Høybråten, the secretary general of Norwegian Church Aid, said at the time the report was released that high debt burdens are 'a huge drain on a country's economy and hits the poorer parts of the population first through cuts in welfare, education, or health expenditure to pay debts.

'A debt crisis is paralysing and undermines all other development efforts.'

As bad as the situation is now, the truth is that the outlook for the future is worse as developing nations face additional pressures such as dealing with the impact of the climate emergency and whatever the next pandemic brings.

But the Global North, unsurprisingly, continues to refuse to do the right thing.

They refuse to pay for the damage they have caused to the planet — impacted most heavily on the world's poorest nations.

The COP29 held in 2024 in the Azerbaijan capital Baku agreed to make available a paltry $300 billion (around £239 billion) for developing countries who need the cash to cope with the transition from coal, oil and gas that causes the globe to overheat. But it is nowhere near the $1.3 trillion (just over a £1 trillion) that developing countries were demanding.

Responding to this, one climate activist from the Global South is alleged to have described the amount being made available as 'not even enough money to pay for the coffins we will need', as people die off from the impacts of climate change.

It is the clearest indication possible that the world's richest nations are interested only in getting richer and do not care about the impoverishment caused by them across huge swathes of the rest of the world.

Unfortunately they have also been able to incorporate some Global South (mis)leaders to maintain these horrendous levels of poverty as a means of controlling working-class and peasant communities.

These so-called leaders have been willing to do the bidding of their masters in the north for the thickening of their personal offshore bank accounts.

To be fair, even many of these leaders appear to understand the basic equation that unless something is done climate change will mean they will actually have no people or country left to 'mislead'.

Those die-hard supporters of the West that remain must be made to understand that it is no longer in their interests to ignore the interests of their own people — millions of whom have no idea from one day to the next how they will put bread on the table and keep a roof over their heads.

In places such as Kenya, more than 90 per cent of the economy is informal with people having to find creative ways to make a living. This is far from unusual across the Global South and means there is no degree of certainty for millions of people over how to survive.

As the massive debt burden continues to bite and the climate emergency adds to the woes of the Global South, survival in this abusive relationship is simply not an option.

Abusive relationships all too often end with the abused being killed.

We need to help organise the intervention into the abusive relationship so the nations being abused can stage a collective getaway.

For decades there have been calls for the debt to be cancelled. We must recharge these calls.

Not only should the debt be cancelled but the debate should be turned into one about how much money these rich nations actually owe the South for the exploitation and the damage they have caused.

The rich nations of the Global North must not be allowed to continue to claim the impracticality of cancelling the debt. There is a precedent for this.

After reversing a decision to keep the defeated Germans impoverished after World War II the western victors instead decided to turn Germany into an economic powerhouse as a bulwark against the Soviet Union.

This led to the cancellation of around 50 per cent of the debt owed by Germany.

They simply do not wish to do the same — at any significant level — for any of the nations of the Global South — around 80 per cent of the global population — that they keep firmly under their iron heel through debt enslavement.

The debate is the wrong way around. We should be talking about the money the rich exploiter countries owe the global south rather than the other way around.

There should be a commitment from the nations of the Global South to agree to stop paying a debt that was forced on them and which, in any case, they can't afford.

There can be no serious progress by the nations of the Global South until debt enslavement is ended.

That requires the leaders in those countries to do what's best for their own populations rather than the transnational corporations that mostly benefit from these high levels of debt and the exploitative relationship with the Global South that it engrains.

But the question remains as to whether the debt owed by Western nations can ever really be repaid.

How can the centuries of exploitation, rape and pillage of the peoples and resources of the continent of Africa ever really be repaid?

Can the fact that I will likely never know exactly who I am descended from ever be compensated? I'm sure that boffins will be able to come up with an approximate sum to account for the hours of free labour during enslavement and colonialism.

Can the forced detachment from our families and the loss of our families, culture and lands — never mind the torture and murder inflicted on Africans — ever actually be monetised? I doubt it very much.

Can a figure be identified that will compensate for the artefacts looted from Africa by the colonial powers? I doubt that too.

But they can make a start on righting the severe wrongs that they have enacted against the people of Africa — wherever they are in the world — who have been left to pick up the pieces after centuries of racism and exploitation.

One of my major annoyances around the debate over debt and reparations is the way that people of African descent are told by white people — including on the left — how best to wage this fight for justice.

They tell us what Africans should legitimately demand in reparations and that the white working class in the belly of the beast should not be made to pay for the excesses of the ruling class.

They say this on the one hand whilst on the other they make it clear that we should always follow the lead of those forces engaged at the head of liberation, socialist or communist movements across the world.

I have to say that being told by white comrades exactly how I as an African should seek justice for the wrongs that have been committed against us is really annoying and deeply disrespectful.

I also don't believe that the white working class should be made to pay for the excesses and exploitation carried out by the ruling class.

The problem is that whatever people of African descent manage to extract from those who still, by the way, profit from slavery, is inevitably going to be passed on through higher prices etc.

One way of bypassing this dilemma is to have a windfall tax on the profits of those entities that can be shown to still be profiting from the legacy of enslavement of Africans.

A mechanism can be worked out for how this windfall tax can be distributed to the descendants of enslavement through cash, grants, scholarships or a range of other mechanisms designed to contribute towards putting right some of the wrongs of the past.

There must also be a commitment to returning the loot stolen from Africa. Many of the artefacts that are now on display in Western museums are where they are because they were stolen from Africa.

Many of these items are precious cultural and religious artefacts that should be in Africa for use — in whatever way the people who they belong to choose.

We do not need advice from museums on how to look after these artefacts — they often say they are worried about how these items will be looked after when they reach home. Not your problem!

Africa is not a place full of primitive savages with no notion of how best to look after our belongings. The continent is as sophisticated as anywhere else on the planet and I am sure capable of working out the best way of taking care of things that are precious to us.

But it is Africa's problem and nobody else's.

Why should we take advice from people who have stolen from us about the best way of taking care of the loot they are returning?

The failure to return the stolen booty to Africa is deeply racist and must end immediately. It is only part of what the former colonial powers who are responsible for this theft should be doing.

The thing that will make the biggest difference to achieving debt justice and reparations is the building of the socialist movements across the Global South that will finally force an end to this wretched enslavement we as Africans still experience.

We must not wait for a Harriet Tubman figure to arrive to lead us out of debt enslavement.

We must organise collectively on an international basis to say enough is enough! We are out of here!

The next chapter on Land talks about the important place the land plays in African culture and how it will play a central role in the rebirth of the continent.

'Poverty is slavery.'

—Proverb from Somalia

CHAPTER THREE — LAND

'**Revolution is based** on land. Land is the basis
of all independence. Land is the basis of freedom,
justice, and equality'

— *Malcolm X*

I HAVE ALWAYS HAD a conflicting relationship with the land.
It took a lot of persuasion to get me to begin working an allotment
that my wife Kate had secured for us.

I was never particularly impressed by the efforts of my dad to grow
spuds in our back garden. At least I never felt the need to help my
dad to do the back-breaking work.

It wasn't just laziness. I think it has a lot to do with my ancestors
being forced to work on the land in a state of enslavement.

When I traced my maternal heritage I found that I am part of a
once nomadic group called the Tikar people from what is
now in Cameroon.

The Tikar people are known as great artists, artisans and storytellers
who are said to have originated from the Nile River Valley in
present-day Sudan.

The Tikar people migrated through what is now Northern Nigeria
to settle in the highlands of western Cameroon. They, like all
Africans, have a spiritual relationship with the land.

This relationship was breached by the Western enslavement of
Africans. But nevertheless, the link to the land was maintained
through bondage even though there would have been a plethora of
methods of celebrating the link with the land depending on where
they were descended.

But one of the things introduced to the Africans during enslavement
and continued through colonisation was the notion that land was a
commodity that could be bought, owned and, if desired, sold.

This very Eurocentric notion of land ownership was as alien to
Africans as it was to indigenous communities throughout the
Global South.

The ownership of property is a core part of capitalist relations with property rights traceable back to the 1215 Magna Carta, which protected the privileges and rights of the nobility against the interference of the state — or the monarch.

In Western Europe, land defined one's wealth and class position. It is little surprise that when colonists arrived in the colonies and stumbled across vast swathes of land, they viewed this as a stroke of fortune and something that they should possess to accumulate wealth.

But for Africans land is neither a commodity nor an individual possession. It doesn't belong to humans but is a gift from the spirits.

Land was understood as a spiritual relationship that brings together the soil, earth and the stars.

African land laws debunk the idea of ownership. Instead land is a natural endowment that can neither be bought nor sold. African land tenure is not based on ownership but on use and access.

Since Africans have common rights to land, communal rights override individual rights, which are subsumed to the overall communal good.

The ancestors belong to the soil, earth and the stars. In African spirituality the ancestors guide and provide support for the living.

One of the things that persuaded me to reconnect to land as an ancestor was discovering the African American land movement and the way that they have managed to incorporate spirituality with food production.

I had believed that I was separate from the land when, in reality, it was always within me as part of my spirit.

Soul Fire Farm, for example, is an Afro-Indigenous-centred community farm and training centre dedicated to uprooting racism and seeding sovereignty in the food system. They prioritise deep reverence for the Earth and wisdom for the ancestors. They practice regenerative farming and work toward food and land sovereignty.

Soul Fire Farm is 80 acres of land that historically was stewarded by the Stockbridge-Munsee Band of the Mohican Nation.

The Mohican people were forcibly removed by the white men and women from their territory in the 1800s to a reservation in northern Wisconsin.

The Farm honours the original stewards of the land through a 'cultural respect easement' which would allow Mohican citizens to use the Soul Fire Land for ceremonies and wildcrafting in perpetuity.

They also have a native seed exchange with some of the farmers and herbalists in the community and are working with Mohican people locally in the fight to preserve their ancestral burial grounds from development.

Soul Fire Farm treats land as an elder member of the family — to be respected and taken care of. This approach draws on the West African heritage of the current stewards to respect the land and to ask the land for permission before making any major changes.

This approach towards the land — as living and breathing — is an ancient heritage but a vital one to maintain and help to flourish if we are to bring about the rebirth of the spirit of Africa to wherever we are in the diaspora.

It also helps us to transcend the flawed economic determinist view current in land debates that denies Africans the right to land on the premise that they would not be able to productively use the land.

For Africans land is everything. Depriving one of land means robbing them of their personhood, being and identity — in other words their full humanity.

Aside from their basic greed and desire to strip Africans of everything that was valuable, the common Western belief system that relegates land to a commodity meant that the reflex of the Europeans was to own the land that did not belong to them. Indeed, to Africans, the land belonged to no one.

This core belief system must be challenged across the diaspora but in Africa, it must be part of the renaissance — the new beginning.

South Africa

The European desire to commodify everything was at the heart of land dispossession and the control of labour in South Africa.

The systematic seizure of African land during the colonial and apartheid eras significantly altered the relationship of the local people to the soil. It turned them into labourers working under exploitative conditions.

The history of this dispossession goes back to the Dutch colonisation of what became known as South Africa in the mid-17th century. When the British took over the mantle of colonial ruler in the 18th century they merely intensified the situation.

At the heart of this land grab was the discovery of rare minerals such as gold and diamonds in the 1880s. These discoveries heightened the demand for cheap African labour that could be exploited so that the Europeans could become richer.

Even after slavery was abolished during the 19th century the colonists introduced laws to regulate the movement of Africans and to determine where they could work and live.

The 1913 Natives Land Act in South Africa was a legislative restriction on the rights of Africans to own land. Some 93 per cent of South African land became off-limits to Africans in their own country. This was now reserved for whites.

Black farmers who had previously owned or rented land in what had been designated 'white areas' were given a choice. They could become labourers — virtual slaves — on white farms or they had to move to 'reserves' the South African government had set aside for them.

These reserves were eventually expanded alongside strict segregation laws.

The formal system of apartheid ran from 1948 to 1994 with land and who could and could not own it at its core.

The homeland system set up by the racist apartheid regime relegated Black South Africans to live in deprived areas and forced them to travel in to work for white South Africans in jobs where for long periods they enjoyed no legal rights in the workplace.

It was not until 1979 that Black trade unions, after years of struggle, were allowed to register with the State and have the right to bargain with employers over terms and conditions in the workplace.

The stealing of African land by the Europeans created a large pool of cheap labour which meant that if the employer wanted to fire a worker there was always someone available to take his or her place working on a pittance wage.

The employment contract, transplanted from colonial law, became a tool for exerting control over these workers. It reinforced their subordinate status.

The homelands ensured a continuous supply of cheap Black migrant labour. This system of land deprivation and labour control not only served the economic interests of the white minority. It also reinforced racial hierarchies.

The legacy of land dispossession in South Africa — along with the control of labour that went with it — continues to shape South Africa's social, economic and political landscape.

The ongoing struggle for land justice is directly linked to this history. Addressing the legacy of dispossession is crucial for economic justice and social stability.

The 2024 Expropriation Act gives the South African government scope to expropriate land from private parties, but only if it's in the public interest and under certain conditions.

This has drawn the ire of United States President Donald Trump and his sidekick South African-born multibillionaire Elon Musk.

Trump accused the South African government of doing 'terrible things' and claimed land was being confiscated from 'certain classes'.

This is clearly untrue and obvious to anyone who cares to even pretend to look. There are even groups in South Africa complaining that no land has actually been expropriated.

The South African government says private property rights are protected and Trump's description of the law is full of misinformation and 'distortions'.

However, the law has prompted concern in South Africa, especially from groups representing parts of the white minority, who say it will target them and their land even though race is not mentioned in the law.

Trump's comments, largely pushed by Musk, who I have yet to hear declare a personal financial interest in the law, are far more likely to do with South Africa's vocal opposition and leadership in the legal fight against the Israeli genocide against the Palestinians in Gaza and role in Brics — with Brazil, Russia, India, China, Indonesia and others.

The new law is clearly tied to the legacy of the racist apartheid system, and colonialism that I have outlined above, and is part of South Africa's efforts to try and find a way to right historical wrongs.

A spokesperson for South Africa's Department of International Affairs said that the misrepresentation of the Land Act 'fuels unwarranted fears' about the targeting of white citizens.

Agri SA, a trade organisation for South African farmers, has also denounced claims of land seizures as 'disinformation'.

The unexpected signing of the Expropriation Act on 23 January 2025 has sparked political turmoil and unnecessary tension within the agri-food system.

'This has been exacerbated by disinformation regarding the Act's intent, impacting negatively on the investment climate for South African agriculture,' Agri SA chief executive Johann Kotzé said.

'To be clear no seizures or confiscations of private property have taken place. Nor has any land been expropriated without compensation. Isolated cases of land grabs and trespassing have been dealt with,' Kotzé added.

Meanwhile, the Solidarity Movement, a network of Afrikaner community institutions that says it represents about 600,000 members, has said it condemns 'the many race laws that make us second-class citizens', including the Expropriation Act and is critical of the ANC's foreign policy.

But it doesn't believe land grabs are taking place.

Whites make up around 7 per cent of South Africa's population of 62 million but own approximately 70 per cent of the private farming land, and the government says that inequality needs to be addressed.

They are entirely correct.

But soon after returning to power as US president Trump issued an executive order to halt hundreds of millions of dollars a year of US aid to South Africa — to help with its response to dealing with HIV/AIDS.

During 2024, the US gave South Africa around $440 million (around £367 million) and funded in the region 17 per cent of South Africa's HIV programme through the President's Emergency Plan for AIDS Relief.

South Africa has around 8 million people living with HIV — with 5.5 million of them receiving antiretroviral medication —

and US funding is vital in supporting the largest national HIV/AIDS programme in the world.

This shows directly the importance of land and the double standards that the West will use to justify its exploitation.

At no time have Trump or Musk or any other world leader made any comment about the fact that this land is African land and it should be for Africans to determine what happens to it.

Zimbabwe

I recall the hysteria that took place when South Africa's neighbour Zimbabwe brought in laws to return land expropriated by whites back to Africans after the country won its liberation.

Land reform policies introduced between 2000 and 2023 were uniformly met with cries of foul by people who had stolen the land from Africans in the first place.

The idea that there was any justice to be had in returning this land to the indigenous community of Africans caused a frenzy across the Western media with white politicians popping up at regular intervals to denounce the actions of the country's leader Robert Mugabe and his Zanu-PF party.

When Robert Mugabe took power in a newly liberated Zimbabwe in 1980, he did what any self-respecting African leader should have done. He brought in a programme to return the land to African Zimbabweans.

The land had been stolen by white farmers who were supporters of the racist Rhodesian regime.

In echoes of my description of the process in South Africa, abundant acres of farmland were reserved for the small white settler population. African Zimbabweans, who comprised the vast majority of the population were restricted to inadequate and less fertile plains.

Initially, a 'willing buyer, willing seller' land reform strategy was introduced. But this was met by an intransigent reluctance of white farmers to part with the land and was hampered by broken promises from Britain to provide inadequate financial assistance for this programme.

The failure of the 'willing buyer willing seller' offer triggered a fast-track land programme in 2000, which saw the seizure of approximately 4,000 white-owned farms for redistribution to African Zimbabweans.

The furore caused by this was all too predictable. This had nothing to do with land justice but, apparently, everything to do with the allegedly evil Marxist Robert Mugabe — who many white commentators were quick to label as a racist.

But some 20 years later, in July 2020, the Zimbabwean government, under the Presidency of Mugabe's successor, Emmerson Mnangagwa announced $3.5 billion (£2.8 billion) in a compensation package for white farmers.

The package, that the country could ill afford, would be paid to the four thousand white Zimbabwean farmers for infrastructure that they had lost.

It was fill your boots time for white farmers when, just a month later in August 2020, it was announced that foreign white farmers who had lost land during the Mugabe land reform programme could apply to get the land back.

At the time, government officials stressed that this grand-scale compensation plan was not a reversal of Zimbabwe's land reform programme, but a 'clarification' and 'correction'.

That's one way of describing it. Another is that it is a complete betrayal of the many thousands of Africans who fought and gave their lives for liberation from colonial rule.

The Zimbabwe government is still attempting to breathe life into the compensation programme. But this is proving difficult as the country, facing heavy sanctions from the West, struggles to kick-start its economy.

Even so the government has managed to find some 20 million dollars (roughly £16 million) to pay as initial compensation to 400 African Zimbabwean farmers and a group of foreign white farmers who lost land during the 2000–2001 land invasions.

President Emmerson Mnangagwa is desperate to mend relations with the West. Over the past two decades, agricultural production has been in freefall.

The violent blow of international sanctions has turned Zimbabwe's green pastures into bleak wastelands. Once an illustrious breadbasket of Africa, Zimbabwe has crumbled.

Zimbabwe's external debt is estimated to be close to $12 billion (£9.6 billion). For 40 per cent of Zimbabweans, food insecurity is a lived experience.

The President appears to have no shame in holding out a begging bowl to the West and going along with the inevitable policy strings that will be attached to any largesse that may come his country's way.

Desperately seeking economic stability and the recovery of the country's agricultural sector, Mnangagwa is using the compensation card as part of his deck to appease Western powers and end US sanctions.

While compensation payments to white farmers may be a sweetener for Western nations, it could well leave a bitter taste for the majority of Zimbabwe Africans who have yet to enjoy even a small patch of land justice.

Mugabe's land reform programme was an incredibly important attempt to reverse the legacy of land theft and dispossession of Africans in Zimbabwe, under colonialism, which saw millions of acres of land made available to white settlers while restricting land to Africans.

Mugabe said at the time: 'The land is ours. It's not European and we have taken it.'

But Mugabe's land strategy was largely strangled at birth by domestic obstacles, including deep tranches of patronage and corruption as well as the extensive international outrage and sanction I mentioned earlier.

There were three key fault lines in the Mugabe land programme. Firstly, it failed to protect agricultural production in the critical phase of land transfer.

Secondly, the key beneficiaries were politically aligned individuals rather than ordinary citizens, creating an ever-greedy political class and an eternally hungry populace.

And thirdly, the rage and retribution of the West were underestimated.

But slowly but surely African farmers are managing to rebuild the tobacco industry, engage in crucial agricultural value chains, and invest in commercial livestock farming and horticulture.

There are many lessons for South Africa and other African nations seeking to bring about land justice.

Great Expectations can turn into hopelessness if land policies and the structure to introduce them are not in place.

There is also the danger that land policies only benefit the elites rather than the people and become areas where corruption and patronage flourish rather than a zone of liberation and equity.

The promise of South Africa's first democratically elected President, Nelson Mandela, that 30 per cent of arable farmland would be transferred back to Africans in the first five years of ANC governance remains a pipe dream. Back in 2022, only 11 per cent had been redistributed.

In addressing the land issue, in both South Africa and Zimbabwe, the real question of compensation should be focused first and foremost on Africans disposed of land in the first instance by whites under colonialism.

That this is not the case is a testament to how the legacy of colonialism and landlessness in Africa is well and kicking.

The Scramble for Africa

The mad, racist 'scramble for Africa,' by European nations was formalised at the Berlin Conference which concluded just over 140 years ago.

The Berlin carve-up of the African continent began on November 15, 1884 and ended with an agreement on February 26, 1885.

European nations, who during the nineteenth century were the planet's dominant powers, were looking for more ways of exploiting Africa's rich resources for their newly growing industrial sectors.

The Europeans were looking to further embed the exploitative trade arrangements that had existed between the two continents for decades. Also, of course, the Europeans had already enslaved millions of Africans to enrich their coffers. Now the Europeans wanted to exercise much more direct control of Africa's rich diversity of natural resources.

There was racist talk about wanting to 'civilise' Africa, but this was in essence part of the justification for the continued horrendous treatment of Africans as free or forced labour.

The reality was that the Europeans wanted the resources and they saw the value in not having to compete — or fight — with each other to get them. But before the Berlin deal they certainly did squabble over who was entitled to what in a continent that was not theirs to argue over.

Britain, Portugal, France, Germany, and King Leopold II of Belgium began sending scouts to secure trade and sovereignty treaties with local leaders, buying or simply staking flags and laying claim to vast expanses of territory crisscrossing the continent rich with resources from palm oil to rubber.

Rows soon broke out between the major powers. The French, for example, clashed with Britain over several West African territories, and again with King Leopold over Central African regions.

To avoid an all-out war over Africa between the rival European nations, all stakeholders agreed to the Berlin meeting to set out common terms and 'manage' the colonisation process.

Needless to say, Africans had no say whatsoever in this. No African nations were invited or represented at the Berlin conference.

On the conference agenda was the clear mapping of an agreement over who owned which region of the continent.

Lines were drawn across Africa that took no notice of traditional or tribal considerations. The only thing that mattered to the Western powers was a carving up of the continent to maximise profit.

Four of the European powers — France, Germany, Britain, and Portugal — already controlled vast swathes of African territory. But others, such as Belgium's King Leopold, also wanted a piece of the action.

Of the 14 nations present at the conference nine left with no territory at all. This reflected the pre-World War I dominance of the Western Europeans.

The countries who went home with empty pockets were Austria-Hungary, Denmark, Russia, Italy, Sweden-Norway, Spain, Netherlands, Ottoman Empire (Turkey) and, notably, the United States.

The carve-up of the African continent internationalised free trade on the Congo and Niger River basins and recognised King Leopold's personally owned International Congo Society.

Leopold claimed he was carrying out humanitarian work. It was an area that became known as the Congo Free State. It would suffer some of the worst brutalities of colonisation ever known, with hundreds of thousands worked to death on rubber plantations, or punished with limb amputations.

The Berlin deal bound all parties to protect the 'native tribes … their moral and material wellbeing,' as well as further suppress the Slave Trade which was officially abolished in 1807/1808, but which was still taking place illegally.

It also stated that merely staking flags on newly acquired territory would not be grounds for ownership, but that 'effective occupation' meant successfully establishing administrative colonies in the regions.

Western 'ownership' of African territories was not finalised at the conference, but after several bilateral events that followed. Liberia was the only country not partitioned because it had gained formal independence from the US.

Ethiopia was briefly invaded by Italy, but resisted colonisation for the most part. After the German and Ottoman empires fell following World War I, a map closer to what we now know as Africa would emerge.

Even that map is portrayed by most cartographers across the West as showing Europe far larger than it is and Africa, of course, far smaller. But the lines drawn on the map have remained largely unchanged since the conference.

Whilst only about 20 per cent of Africa — mainly the coastal parts of the continent — had already been claimed by European powers as theirs before the conference, by 1890 about 90 per cent of African territory was colonised, including inland nations.

The conference did not begin the process of colonisation in Africa but it certainly accelerated the process.

But what was the impact of the conference in real terms?

Whilst it meant the next stage in the rape, looting and pillaging of Africa and the erasing of African culture it did not mean the end of resistance to colonial rule.

From the first instance of the exploitation of Africans and the racism used to justify it, there has been resistance.

This racism has not just disappeared as the world has moved on to the next stage of imperialist domination of Africa. It has continued to impact the way that the Western powers treat Africa.

The same racism that enabled the Western powers to carve up the African continent without consideration for Africans is the same racism that allows Africa to be treated today as a mere extraction zone and its people as cheap labour to secure the valuable minerals needed to maintain Western wealth.

It is all too easy to see events such as the Berlin conference as being so far away in history that it bears no relation to events of today. Nothing could be further from the truth.

The identification of Africans as inferior to whites stems from enslavement and colonialism. The West continues to reap the benefits of those supremacist beliefs today.

If Africa is to arise from the exploitation of the West then it must reclaim its history and with it pride in Africa as a continent and Africans as a people.

I think the story of the remaining three quarters of the 21st century will be the rise of Africa and Africans on the continent as well as across the diaspora.

Part of this rebirth must be a reclamation of Africa by removing the lines imposed on the continent at the Berlin conference.

Without this, the debate about the future of Africa will continue to take place within the constraints created by those who led the racist scramble for the continent at the Berlin conference.

The very beautiful, rich and diverse continent of Africa needs to be brave enough to shift the paradigm and kickstart its future on its own terms.

'If two brothers fight over their father's land, it is a stranger who will enjoy their sweat and labour.'

— *African proverb*

CHAPTER FOUR — BREAD

'**Rather a piece** of bread with a happy heart than wealth with grief.'

— *African proverb.*

I WAS BROUGHT UP by my parents to enjoy food and to share it. Not just what was left over — but whatever I had.

As in most West Indian households there was always food on the stove. It was, of course, there for us kids but it was also cooked so that anyone who visited could eat if they so wished.

Friends of my parents — including people we called uncle or aunt out of respect for our elders often visited during an evening or particularly on a Saturday to enjoy one of my mom or dad's curries or fried fish or chicken.

This was just normal and something that was brought over to Britain from Jamaica. There was a basic principle at play that anyone who was in our orbit and needed food would always get it.

This wasn't because we as a family had loads of money — we did not. It was to do with a culture that developed over many centuries — before, during and after enslavement — that prioritised looking after your friends and neighbours.

What has become known as Jamaican food is actually a rich mix of different influences.

Prior to the arrival of the Europeans and the enslaved Africans what became known as Jamaica was the home of the Taino people — as far as we know the first known inhabitants of the island.

It was the culinary practices of the Taino people that laid the foundation for what we now regard as traditional Jamaican dishes.

The Taino had a rich diet that included fish, meats, fruits and vegetables that were either grilled or baked in earth ovens.

Perhaps the most famous cooking method passed down from the Taino is 'jerking', which involves seasoning meat with a blend of spices and cooking it over a pimento wood fire.

The forced arrival of enslaved Africans transformed and enriched the food on the island. But the cooking methods used by the Taino also became part of the resistance movement against the colonisers.

Maroons in Jamaica are descendants of enslaved Africans who managed to liberate themselves and established free communities in the mountainous regions of the island.

They are said to have preserved meat using jerk seasoning while evading the colonists who were attempting to hunt them down in the mountains.

In between their battle for survival on the plantations of Jamaica, the enslaved Africans brought with them a rich heritage of utilising bold spices and multiple uses of staples such as yams, plantains and okra — which West Africans introduced to the island.

Enslaved Africans had to improvise with the scraps from their masters' tables. Europeans frequently assigned them the parts of animals considered unsuitable for consumption.

As a result, this led to the development of unique cooking techniques, such as slow cooking, seasoning, and smoking, to make these tough cuts of meat more palatable.

One of the most popular ingredients in Jamaican cuisine with African roots is okra, which people often use in stews and soups.

Okra was used extensively in African cooking to thicken stews and soups.

Arguably the biggest African influence on food on the island is in the country's national dish ackee and saltfish. Ackee is a fruit native to West Africa and was brought over by traders as well as smuggled in by enslaved Africans.

Enslaved Africans also brought across their practice of using all parts of the animal destined for the pot — including offal. This led to the creation of dishes such as 'mannish water' (a goat soup) and 'cow foot stew'.

My particular thanks to the enslaved Africans is for the taste I have inherited from them for very hot peppers and spices. For that — alongside so many other things — my ancestors receive my eternal gratitude.

Whilst the African diaspora in Jamaica is able to point back to the Mother continent for its food heritage it would be wrong not to acknowledge that there have been other food influences.

The Spanish, the first colonisers of Jamaica, introduced pigs and cattle to the island. They also brought with them the wider use of frying and roasting food as well as ingredients such as citrus fruits and sugar cane. Both of these became central to the economy of Jamaica — which I will return to in later chapters.

The British, who ousted the Spanish in 1707, also had a major influence on the food in Jamaica. The British influenced the creation of the Jamaican 'patty', a pastry filled with spiced meat or vegetables.

When indentured labourers were brought from India to the Island in the 19th century Jamaican cuisine diversified yet further as curry powder and turmeric became more widely used and helped to create dishes such as 'curried goat' and 'curried chicken'. They also introduced dishes that are now staples such as roti (a flatbread).

The Rastafarian movement has also been an important influence on the food culture of the island and yet another fusion between Jamaica's native and African cultures.

The Rastafari movement began in Jamaica in the 1930s as a religious and cultural movement among the descendants of enslaved Africans.

Rastafarians promote a natural lifestyle, emphasising vegetarianism and an 'Ital' diet.

The Ital diet is plant-based and adheres to the Rastafarian belief in natural living. The word 'Ital' is derived from the word 'vital', emphasising the importance of eating foods that are natural and in their purest form.

Continuing the theme that is at the heart of Jamaica's national motto 'Out of Many, One People', Rastafarian food is a fusion of African, Caribbean, and Asian culinary traditions, using fresh fruits, vegetables, and herbs to create nutrient-rich dishes.

In Jamaican Ital Cuisine, people commonly use ingredients like callaloo (a leafy green vegetable), yams, cassava, and plantains. They often season dishes with herbs and spices such as ginger, garlic, and thyme.

I have taken the time to explain the food influences in Jamaica to show that the influences on the diaspora have never been one-dimensional or static. It is always evolving and drawing on influences from across the globe.

But the diaspora has managed to maintain a core connection to the African continent because of the survival techniques used by enslaved Africans.

Africans needed to find ways of eating the scraps thrown at them like dogs by the slavers so they developed new techniques of preserving food and ways of flavouring and cooking food to make it more edible.

Of course some of these techniques would have been known to the Africans before enslavement and used in their homes. But there can be little doubt that the necessity of survival meant that Africans were forced to innovate. Many of these survival techniques are not considered expensive delicacies with rich restaurateurs across the globe charging a pretty penny for food that was once created from the scraps of the slavers.

The continent of Africa itself is home to literally hundreds of different cultural and ethnic groups each with their own culinary traditions and cooking techniques.

The scientists still believe that eastern and southern Africa were home to the planet's first humans.

In *Africans: The History of a Continent* (1995), the author John Iliffe argues that there is evidence as long as 20,000 years ago 'of intensive exploitation of tubers and fish at waterside settlements in southern Egypt.'

This, he says, was followed by the 'collecting of wild grains', such as sorghum, pearl millet, finger millet, African rice and teff.

That's just around Egypt in the northeast of the continent.

One can consider the size of the continent of Europe and the differences in food preferences travelling from one nation to another. When this is compared to the continent of Africa — roughly three times larger than Europe — one can begin to understand the scale of diversity of foods and tastes that exist.

Climate and location make a huge difference to the food that is available.

The African continent has a rich biodiversity, thriving across various climates from the Sahara's edges to the lush rainforests and vibrant coastlines.

This does not just create a diversity of conditions for different crops to grow but it also means that each region has different skill sets with some being expert farmers in certain crops whilst others are better at growing other items, herding or catching fish.

I will return to this in the chapter on *Work*.

Archaeological sites in Ghana show that hunter-gatherers moved around the forests and savannas of the region in the period 1750 to 1350 BC. They ate a wide variety of foods including tortoises, lizards, turtles and snails.

In South Africa domestic crops grown during the Iron Age included millet and sorghum — which prefer a well-drained soil not available in some parts of the continent.

These two examples alone should serve to illustrate that tastes developed alongside what was available and the type of soil conditions in the area.

Food — or the lack thereof — in Africa must never be seen as purely a local phenomenon that has no influence from outside sources. It is a highly political and economic dynamic that has sometimes been used to demonstrate the wealth and well-being of a country. At other times it is also a reflection of geopolitical dynamics.

During the 20th century, cities in northern Nigeria were able to show off what became known as 'groundnut pyramids'. These even became tourist attractions.

Before oil was discovered in Nigeria, agriculture was the backbone of the nation's economy, with groundnut (peanuts) as one of its most prominent cash crops.

In the northern region of the country, particularly in Kano, groundnut production thrived and became a symbol of economic wealth and cultural pride.

The famous groundnut pyramids of Kano, each containing around 15,000 sacks, stood tall as a testament to Nigeria's agricultural boom during the 1960s and early 1970s. Kano was once renowned for its magnificent groundnut pyramids, a hallmark of the agricultural prosperity that dominated Nigeria's economy before the oil era.

At its peak, Nigeria produced 41 per cent of the total groundnut output in West Africa, with Kano, at one time Nigeria's most populous state with around 10 million people, serving as the epicentre of this thriving trade.

The pyramids, often towering higher than the surrounding buildings, were a source of pride for northern Nigeria and a key driver of the region's economy.

Groundnut farming gained prominence in 1912, fuelled by the crop's high economic value. At the end of each growing season, agents from marketing boards visited farms across the region to purchase produce, while some farmers transported their goods directly to Kano.

Once collected, the groundnuts were shipped via train to Lagos for export, underscoring the strategic role of agriculture in Nigeria's global trade network.

But, the golden era of groundnut pyramids began to fade in the mid-1970s. By 1973, Nigeria's total groundnut production, which had peaked at over 1.6 million tons, had dropped significantly to less than 700,000 tons by the 1980s.

The decline was attributed to various factors, including a shift by farmers and traders to alternative crops like cowpea, sorghum, and millet.

This downturn had a cascading effect on industries reliant on groundnut as a raw material. Many factories were forced to close or transition to other sources of oil, marking the end of an era for Kano's iconic pyramids.

The groundnut pyramids were the brainchild of Alhaji Alhassan Dantata, the wealthiest man in West Africa during the 1940s.

Each pyramid he built contained 15,000 sacks of groundnuts, embodying his vision of economic prosperity. Interestingly, his great-grandnephew, Alhaji Aliko Dangote, would go on to become the world's richest Black man, continuing the family legacy of entrepreneurship and success.

Today, the groundnut pyramids of Kano are remembered as a proud chapter in Nigeria's agricultural history. They serve as a reminder of the country's potential for diversification and the wealth that lies in its agricultural heritage.

Kano State has since become a flashpoint for conflict between

Nigeria and the Jihadist group Boko Haram — discussed further in the chapter called *Peace*.

Zimbabwe was once known as the breadbasket of Africa for its exports of crops such as cotton, maize and sugarcane. Yam festivals across West Africa — from Nigeria to Ghana and Benin and beyond — are examples of how the economy and culture are food intersections on the African continent.

From the development of international trade routes through Africa in the 15th century to the creation of cash-crop economics and the loss of indigenous markets in the 19th century, there have been extraordinary shifts in food culture on the continent.

European colonists in countries like Uganda and Kenya practised burning crops and killing livestock as part of their attempts to quell rebellions against their rule.

By leasing the most fertile lands, displacing the local population and forcing them into labour, they disrupted traditional food systems.

What little wages were paid often came in the form of sacks of maize, which soon became the main source of crop.

This replaced more traditional farming crops like millet, tubers, legumes, and kale, which provided a more versatile and nutrient-rich diet. The supplanting of indigenous crops has inevitably contributed to a diminishment in global food systems.

More recently, industrialisation has had an impact on food culture, with an increase in the importation of processed foods and fast food.

Changing consumption patterns such as the rapidly growing fast food culture across parts of the continent have been attributed to rapid urbanisation & a growing middle class.

But the displacement of rural farmers and the proliferation of city slums have combined to create a cycle of greater food insecurity and heavy reliance on imports, including cheaper, energy-dense, and fatty fast food options.

Traditional food sources have dwindled The desire of younger workers to find work drive migration as hunger mounts in almost all African sub-region.

At around 20 per cent, Africa has the highest level of undernourishment in the world.

The coexistence of undernutrition with rising rates of obesity — known as the double burden of malnutrition — creates a paradox of heightened malnutrition and increasing food insecurity across the continent.

Over-reliance on commodities like oil as the mainstay of economies in countries has also led to less financial support for manufacturing, processing, and scale of knowledge across the agricultural supply chain.

The Covid-19 pandemic has increased the challenges facing Africans. The lockdowns meant there was a shortage of workers able to do the wide range of activities necessary for food production.

But Africa is still not short of food. This assertion is actually utterly bogus.

One can easily get misdirected — as if in some magic show by the statistics usually readily on offer.

Around 67.4 million people in the Horn of Africa are food insecure, according to the Food and Agriculture Organisation of the United Nations (FAO) and the Intergovernmental Authority on Development (IGAD).

Of the 67.4 million people, 38 million live in the IGAD member states, including Djibouti, Ethiopia, Kenya, Somalia, South Sudan, Sudan and Uganda.

The rest are in the other countries that make up the Horn of Africa, including the Central African Republic and the Democratic Republic of the Congo (DRC).

'Conflict remains the dominant driver of East Africa's food crisis, with about 38 million people across the IGAD region facing high levels of acute food insecurity,' the institutions noted, adding that extreme weather and climate shocks have become more severe and frequent, driving food insecurity.

According to the two organisations, the region is home to more than 29 million displaced individuals as a result of both conflict and climate-related risks, mainly in Sudan and the DRC.

The report said the displacement of the population is negatively affecting the food security situation of many host communities by putting additional pressure on their resources.

Interventions to prevent and treat malnutrition and diseases are needed, and if not addressed in a timely manner, high rates of mortality will likely occur.

The United Nations Office for the Coordination of Humanitarian Affairs has noted that frequent climate shocks and conflict are worsening poverty and acute food insecurity and malnutrition in Horn Africa.

Massive flooding in Nigeria and Chad in recent years has made the situation acute.

Although the numbers are staggering, the new report reduces last year's estimate of the number of people facing food insecurity by 7.7 million.

The World Food Programme (WFP) attributes the drop to better-than-average rainfall and marginal security improvements, which are unlikely to continue improving.

The WFP report says food insecurity will next year touch nearly one in ten people in West and Central Africa which the World Bank estimates is home to over half a billion people.

Margot van der Velden, WFP's regional director for Western Africa, said the 'vicious cycle of hunger' in the region can be broken with better planning and preparedness.

'We need timely, flexible, and predictable funding to reach crisis-affected people with lifesaving assistance, and massive investments in preparedness, anticipatory action and resilience-building to empower communities and reduce humanitarian needs,' said Van der Velden.

Sudan, which has been gripped by a civil war since April 2023 is regarded as the scene of the world's biggest humanitarian crisis.

The leading cause of death across Sudan is preventable disease and starvation.

Experts are warning that some 25 million of the country's 42 million population are expected to face acute hunger during 2025.

It is just impossible to get full access to the country to get true figures on the full scale of the catastrophe that is taking place but aid workers on the ground say the civil war in Sudan has created the world's worst humanitarian crisis, with many thousands at risk of famine.

Food is not mere sustenance for Africans. It is often a family or spiritual matter. Either way, the continent has food in abundance to feed its population.

One of the problems is the way that working-class and peasant communities have been priced out of being able to buy basic foods as the needs of monopoly capital take precedence over the needs of the people.

Africa needs to regain its food sovereignty if it is ever to stand up as a genuinely free and independent continent able to chart its own future. But the climate emergency will play a key role in determining this.

> **'When you invite someone** to sit at your table and you want to cook for them, you're inviting a person into your life.'
>
> — *Maya Angelou*

CHAPTER FIVE — WATER

'**A fool and water** will go the way they are diverted.'

— African proverb

I OFTEN WONDER whether referring to 'Mother Earth' makes it easier or at least more familiar for the men who run the world to inflict the violence on the planet that they do.

Given the levels of violence directed at women across the world by men, I do wonder whether the violent assault on the planet is a part of the same process.

You can't ever talk about Africa as if it were one country. The climate across this vast continent is incredibly diverse.

North Africa is very hot with a desert climate without much rain. Although temperatures are generally very high, they can drop to below freezing in the mountains and the Sahara desert at night.

The climate of North Africa is dominated by the Sahara desert which around 11,000 years ago, was covered in plant life. It is also known to have even had a 'megalake' that covered over 42,000 square miles.

Equatorial Africa, mostly known as Central Africa, has a monsoon climate with high temperatures and humidity with heavy seasonal rains.

East Africa has separate dry and rainy seasons. Separate dry and rainy seasons happen in most countries south of the Sahara Desert, instead of the traditional spring, summer, autumn and winter seasons of Europe and the US.

The weather in Southern Africa varies more than its northern neighbours, with the temperature changing considerably throughout the year.

This is a very large region, so it has a diverse climate all to itself.

Winters in South Africa are cold and windy with harsh winds, and summers are warmer but with heavy rains.

The seasons are, of course, reversed from the Northern Hemisphere, because summer lasts from November to January and winter runs from June to August.

Savannas are mostly made up of grass and a few sparse trees. The African Savanna spans over about half of Africa.

The savanna grassland's climate is usually warm, with temperatures ranging from 20 to 30°C (68° to 86°F). The African savanna weather has summers that are regarded as the wet season — however still warm.

Temperatures throughout the summer season stay above 27 degrees Celsius. Evaporated heat coming from moisture near the Earth, elevates up and merges with the moisture in the air above, which is cooler.

Savannas usually form in areas where there's a dry winter season for four to six months, and a wet summer season for six to eight months.

Traditionally, during the driest month for African savanna weather, precipitation is less than sixty millimetres.

In the southern hemisphere, rain falls around October to March, and in the northern hemisphere, it falls around May to September. African Savanna weather has annual rainfall that reaches ten to thirty inches per year.

During the savanna's dry season, there are frequent lightning strikes, which hit the ground and ignite the dry grasses, which spread fires over the area. In fact, Africa's savanna weather causes fires that make up the largest portion (71 per cent) of areas burned in the world.

All of what I have just described is changing because of the climate emergency plunging humans, animals and crops into a period of dangerous change.

By 2030, it is estimated that up to 118 million extremely poor people (living on less than £1.50 per day) will be exposed to drought, floods and extreme heat in Africa, if adequate response measures are not put in place.

This will place additional burdens on poverty alleviation efforts and significantly hamper growth, according to figures cited in the report.

Over the past 60 years, Africa has observed a warming trend that has become more rapid than the global average.

In 2024, the continent experienced deadly heat waves, heavy rains, floods, tropical cyclones, and prolonged droughts.

Many countries in the Horn of Africa, southern and North West Africa continued to suffer exceptional multi-year drought, other countries experienced extreme precipitation events during 2024 which led to flooding with significant casualties.

These changing patterns of extreme weather in Africa have continued into 2025.

Parts of southern Africa have been gripped by damaging drought. Exceptional seasonal rainfall has caused death and devastation in East African countries, most recently in Sudan and South Sudan.

Africa is already experiencing a desperate humanitarian crisis caused by the climate emergency.

Temperatures: In Africa, 2023 was in the top three warmest years in the 124-year record, depending on the dataset used. The mean temperature was 0.61° C higher than the 1991–2020 average and 1.23° C above the 1961–1990 long-term baseline.

The African continent has been warming at a slightly faster rate than the global average, at about +0.3 °C per decade between 1991 and 2023.

The warming has been most rapid in North Africa, around +0.4 °C per decade between 1991 and 2023, compared to +0.2 °C/decade between 1961 and 1990. Southern Africa experienced the lowest warming trend compared to the other sub-regions, around +0.2 °C/decade between 1991 and 2023.

The highest temperature anomalies in 2023 were recorded across northwestern Africa, especially in Morocco, coastal parts of Mauritania and northwest Algeria.

Several countries including Mali, Morocco, United Republic of Tanzania, and Uganda reported their warmest year on record in 2023. Extreme heat waves in July and August affected northern Africa. Tunis, the capital of Tunisia reached a record of 49°C and Agadir, Morocco reached a new maximum temperature of 50.4°C.

Regions with a marked rainfall deficit included the western part of North and Northwestern Africa, the Horn of Africa, portions of Southern Africa including Zambia, Zimbabwe, Botswana, and most of Namibia. In addition, Madagascar, central Sudan, northern

Ethiopia and Uganda suffered from below-normal precipitation.

West Africa experienced a normal to early onset of its monsoon rainy season in 2023. Rainfall was notably higher than normal in Angola and coastal areas north of the Gulf of Guinea.

Sea-level rise: The rate of sea-level rise around Africa was close to or slightly higher than the global mean rate of 3.4 mm per year. The largest rate of sea level rise was observed in the Red Sea, reaching 4.1 mm per year.

Extreme climate events

At least 4,700 confirmed deaths in Libya were attributed to flooding following the Mediterranean cyclone 'Storm Daniel' in September 2023, with 8,000 still missing.

Parts of Kenya, Somalia and Ethiopia experienced widespread and severe flooding, with more than 350 deaths and 2.4 million displaced people during the April-June rainy season.

Record-breaking tropical Cyclone Freddy caused extensive flooding during the final landfall, both in Mozambique and Malawi, as extremely heavy rain fell (up to 672 mm during the storm in Mozambique). Malawi was especially hard hit with at least 679 deaths reported. A further 165 deaths were reported in Mozambique.

Severe flooding with associated landslides affected central Africa in early May on the border between Rwanda and the Democratic Republic of Congo, killing at least 574 people.

The White Nile in South Sudan reached record-high levels in February. Basic needs such as food, clean water, and healthcare were difficult to access and there was a near-total collapse of local livelihoods.

In September and October, approximately 300,000 people were affected by flooding across 10 countries, with Niger, Benin, Ghana and Nigeria most heavily impacted.

Parts of Morocco, Algeria, Tunisia, Nigeria, Cameroon, Ethiopia, Madagascar, Angola, Zambia, Zimbabwe and the Democratic Republic of Congo experienced severe drought in 2023.

Zambia faced its worst drought in the last 40 years, affecting eight out of ten provinces and approximately six million people.

Despite all evidence to the contrary some politicians still try to insist that the emergency facing the climate is somehow a figment of our collective imagination.

Nowhere is the emergency more apparent than across the Global South and Africa is a case in point.

Experts point to overwhelming evidence that the African continent is warming faster than the rest of the world (see the State of the Climate in Africa report). They say things are so bad that within just a few short years Africa could lose all of its glaciers.

Within years Mount Kenya could become one of the world's first major mountain ranges to entirely lose its glaciers.

Not that you would have heard this reported anywhere in the mainstream media.

Discussing this might start to raise more questions than the ruling elite are prepared to answer. Questions such as: How did this happen? Who is to blame? How can we fix it?

The year 2024 saw deadly heat waves taking hold across West Africa and the Sahel region of the continent. There are few experts who try to argue that these events are anything other than human-induced.

Namibia was forced to declare a state of emergency during May of 2024 as the country suffered the worst drought in a century. The government even planned to kill wild animals so that the meat from those beasts could be distributed to the many thousands of people who simply had no food.

Namibia wasn't alone. It was just one of several nations across southern Africa that found themselves struggling to cope with devastating drought conditions.

An indication of the changing climate was the way the Sahara — the largest desert in the world but pre-historically a vast sea — faced flooding for the first time in half a century.

In January, Hurricane Belal slammed into the Indian Ocean island of Mauritius.

Later in March, Cyclone Gamane ravaged another African Indian Island nation, Madagascar, forcing 20,737 people to flee.

In May, Hurricane Hidaya devastated coastal regions of the East African nations of Kenya and Tanzania.

The Democratic Republic of Congo (DRC) was hit by heavy downpours.

The DRC has seen people, homes and roads washed away by torrents of rain.

The much relied-on rainy season in the Sahel, from July to September saw heavy flooding, especially in Sudan, Nigeria, Niger, Chad, and the land of part of my heritage, Cameroon.

Of Africans living in coastal areas, about 30 million live in areas considered flood hazard zones.

Flooding is, of course, not entirely due to the climate emergency. Many cities in Africa are poorly planned and have inadequate infrastructure to cope with the rapid urbanisation taking place as people try to escape rural poverty.

But even the increasing rural poverty in many African nations comes about because of the impact of the worsening climate emergency.

The scarcity of water throws up a number of other issues that rarely get mentioned in Africa or elsewhere.

The main water carriers across the world are women. If water becomes scarce in one area it usually means that they have to walk further to find water for their families before bringing the supply back home.

During the severe drought in Morocco in 2022 the authorities failed to provide adequate assistance to indigenous communities that have relied on particular water sources for generations.

As conditions worsened indigenous communities reported feeling abandoned by the authorities.

It seems the further away indigenous communities are from the centres of power the less likely it is that they will receive assistance from governments often more concerned to maintain favour with the western nations that are the main causes of the climate emergency through their carbon emissions.

A report at the end of last year by the European Union's Copernicus Climate Change Service said temperatures had risen by 0.14 degrees Centigrade.

In Zambia, the rainy season—typically running from October to March—ended early in January, as a direct result of extreme heat.

The world's newest nation, South Sudan, saw temperatures reach 45 degrees C, forcing the government to close schools for the first time.

The climate emergency is having a dire impact on agriculture, on which around 70 per cent of Southern Africa's population depend for their livelihoods.

In October, Lesotho, Malawi, Namibia, Zambia, and Zimbabwe all declared their hunger crises as national disasters.

According to the United Nations World Food Programme around 21 million children in Southern Africa are currently malnourished due to failed crops.

The Conference of the Parties

The 2024 Conference of the Parties (COP29) held in Baku Azerbaijan led to delegates agreeing to $300 billion (£327.5 billion) by 2035 to support developing nations to deal with the climate crisis.

For a few years now, the intersection between climate change on human health has been gaining traction. Climate finance has been at the heart of the discussions.

Africa stands at a crossroads, bearing the brunt of climate change's impacts despite contributing minimally to global emissions. Climate change is not just an environmental crisis; it is a public health emergency, especially in Africa.

For many negotiators from Africa COP29 was an utter disaster.

More useful and far more important than my view from Babylon are the thoughts on the outcome from the people who are being forced to live through the disastrous aftermath of another failed climate conference.

Iskander Erzini Vernoit, executive director of the Imal Initiative for Climate and Development, a think tank based in Rabat, Morocco, called Baku a betrayal of the world's vulnerable, of the Paris Agreement, and of common sense.

She said: 'The COP29 decision on the new finance goal represents a staggering lack of imagination and solidarity from the Global North.

'This decision jeopardises the delivery of the aims of the Paris Agreement and UN Framework Convention, throwing national climate target-setting and delivery into deep uncertainty.'

Evans Njewa, the Chair of the Least Developed Countries (LDC) Group at UN Climate Change negotiations, said: 'The LDC Group is outraged and deeply hurt by the outcome of COP29.

'Once again, the countries most responsible for the climate crisis have failed us. This is not just a failure; it is a betrayal.'

She added: 'It sacrifices the needs of the world's poorest and most vulnerable to protect the narrow interests of those who created this crisis. It prioritises profits and convenience over survival and justice.'

Fadhel Kaboub, an associate professor of economics at Denison University and president of the Global Institute for Sustainable Prosperity, said: 'Unless the Global South recognises that we need to create geopolitical leverage to pressure the historic polluters to act differently, we will continue to lose in every single multilateral space.

'We are the global majority. We can leverage the complementarity of our resources and capabilities to impose a new international economic order of justice, peace, and prosperity.'

Professor Kaboub added: 'No progress will be made in COP30 unless the Global South creates the geopolitical leverage it needs to level the playing field.'

Campaign and Policy lead at Climate Action Network (CAN) Africa, Wafa Misrar, said: 'Africa will not back down. We will continue to hold the line until we see meaningful commitments that respect our rights, futures and dignity. The world cannot afford to lose Africa. And we cannot afford to lose ourselves again.'

Ali Mohamed was the Chair of the African Group of Negotiators (AGN) during the negotiations. He said 'Africa demanded clear targets for mitigation, adaptation and loss & damage management. We received none.'

He said: 'Our task now is to translate words into action. Substantial finance flows must reach those on the frontlines — families forced to flee rising seas, farmers facing failed crops, and communities recovering from cyclones.'

Thato Gabaitse, the Development & Administrative Director at WE, The World said this was a reminder that the system is designed to protect wealth, not justice.

He said: 'Developed nations continue to exploit the resources, labour, and goodwill of the Global South while avoiding their historical responsibility for the climate crisis.

'The promise of a "just transition" becomes an empty phrase as fossil fuel dependency deepens to meet debt-servicing obligations.'

Director of Power Shift Africa, Mohamed Adow, said rich countries had managed to stage a great escape in their betrayal of people and the planet.

He said Baku was 'a disaster for the developing world. Sadly, it has been a betrayal of both people and planet by wealthy countries who claim to take climate change seriously.

'Part of the problem was how shamefully the hosts Azerbaijan led the summit. It has been a global embarrassment for the wealthy countries, and the COP president that allowed them to dodge their obligations.'

The basic problem is that the COP process has become a staggering waste of everyone's time and energy.

I do not believe there is a single person — on any side of the negotiations during the COP meetings that really believes anything meaningful and life-saving will emerge.

The COP process has descended into performance with Global North ministers queuing up to be captured on camera crying because they have just saved the world (see Tory chair of the conference Alok Sharma at the end of the equally unproductive COP26 in Glasgow in 2021).

Relying on these conferences for the rich nations of the Global North to do the right thing seems to me to be nothing short of wishful thinking. It is simply not in their economic and political interests to do so. If it was, they would have done something.

I am not arguing to abandon the process and continuing to try to force these nations to fulfil the obligations they have made as well as make restitution for the environmental damage they have largely caused. But other ways must be found to tackle the environmental crisis that is already hitting Africa hard.

Fossil Fuel Non-Proliferation Treaty

Oil giant Shell has been drilling for oil in the Niger Delta since 1956. In the process they have destroyed the way of life of farmers and folks that rely on fishing to seek out a living.

A community of over two million people has had their land, air, and water contaminated. It was during protests over this murder of the environment that writer and human rights activist Ken Saro-Wiwa was hanged in 1995.

Some 30 years later, Shell spills about 40 million litres of oil every year across the Niger Delta and has poisoned the land with heavy metals such as chromium, lead, and mercury, and many young people have turned to crime to survive.

Nigeria produces 1.5 million barrels of oil per day, contributing to Shell's enormous profits. Meanwhile, life expectancy for the people of the Niger Delta is barely 45 years.

Nigeria, despite its rich oil reserves, is desperately poor with some 87 million Nigerians living below the poverty line. After India, Nigeria has the world's second-largest population of poor people.

These patterns are replicated across Africa, where oil and gas have destroyed the way of life of countless communities.

In Angola, the second largest oil-producing country in sub-Saharan Africa, people also live in abject poverty. 1.55 million barrels of oil per day have not turned the people into millionaires. Instead, Angola has one of the highest mortality rates associated with air pollution in the world.

It is also worth noting that it is estimated that more Africans were enslaved from the area now known as Angola than anywhere else on the continent.

The bottom line is that fossil fuels — the main cause of the climate crisis facing the planet — can only be stopped if the drilling is stopped, and there is a transition to clean energy.

One way of doing this would be for all African governments to support the Fossil Fuel Non-Proliferation Treaty, which calls for an end to new coal, oil, and gas projects and demands a justice-based energy transition.

This should be treated by African nations with even more importance than the Nuclear Non-Proliferation Treaty is treated. For Africans, it deals with the same existential threat to existence.

It is a bold proposal grounded in global justice and equity that is premised on the basic fact that fossil fuels are fuelling climate breakdown. Coal, oil and gas are responsible for nearly 90 per cent of the carbon emissions. The world's wealthiest countries have succeeded in bringing our planet to her knees and placing the lives of Africans on the line.

Nothing new here. The rich colonial powers have never respected Africa or Africans for anything other than the wealth we can accumulate for them.

For any lasting solution, we must go to the root. The Fossil Fuel Non-Proliferation Treaty Initiative does this by proposing an international mechanism for change.

It attempts to drive three big shifts.

It wants to see an end to fossil fuel expansion globally, a fair phase out of existing extraction, with the richest nations who have driven the climate catastrophe phasing out first and fastest and providing technical and financial support to developing nations.

It also wants a financed just transition that facilitates energy access, economic diversification, renewable energy deployment, and alternative development pathways.

The push for a Fossil Fuel Non-Proliferation Treaty is spearheaded by a bloc of 16 Global South nations — including two fossil fuel producers — from the Pacific, Latin America and the Caribbean, and Southeast Asia.

African nations need to become part of this growing movement of 120 cities, 3,500 organisations and institutions including the European Parliament, more than 3000 scientists and academics, 101 Nobel laureates and the World Health Organisation.

This impressive list is also joined by hundreds of trade unions representing 30 million workers in more than 150 countries.

This proposal for justice is more necessary than ever for our people. As a continent, our carbon emissions have been negligible, yet, as I showed earlier in this chapter, Africa suffers from a growing number of cyclones, floods and droughts that have been driven by the greed of fossil fuel corporations.

The experience of Angola, Nigeria, and many more countries, demonstrates how the continued use of fossil fuels benefits multinationals while millions of Africans are energy-poor as their communities, culture, and food sources are destroyed.

Many experts are clear that unless this is tackled the number of conflicts in Africa over food and water will escalate as people fight over increasingly scarce resources.

The Democratic Republic of Congo is one of the most fertile countries in the world. Experts say the Congo River has the highest hydroelectric potential in Africa.

The Congo Basin, known as the 'lungs of Africa', is the largest carbon sink in the world, absorbing more carbon than the Amazon and providing a critical habitat for endangered species.

But if the DRC continues oil drilling, the beauty and the carbon sink will be destroyed and more wars and famine will follow.

Many argue that the fighting in the eastern DRC between the Congolese government and the Rwanda-backed M23 militia is the start of this process. They argue that for all their protestations of non-involvement, Rwanda is battling to take control of the rare earth minerals including oil that are abundant in that part of the country.

If Africa continues to do the same things and expects to see different results there will be many disappointed people. Many others will have had their death sentences confirmed.

Health

Tens of millions of Africans are already experiencing the detrimental health effects of climate change.

From heat stress and extreme weather events to the increased spread of infectious diseases, the continent faces a dual crisis: climate change and health vulnerabilities.

The WHO warns that between 2030 and 2050, climate change is expected to cause an additional 250,000 deaths annually due to malnutrition, malaria, diarrhoea, and heat stress.

These figures highlight a grim reality — Africa's health sector, already under-resourced and overburdened, is ill-equipped to manage the growing threats posed by climate change.

The global community must recognise this as a health crisis, not just an environmental one, and act swiftly to mitigate its impacts.

The Lancet report from 2023, Countdown on Health and Climate Change, climate change is widening health inequalities.

The report also said this was disproportionately affecting the most vulnerable populations. Africa falls into that category but perhaps more so as it warms faster than the global average.

As Africa faces a complex range of population and health challenges due to climate change, understanding these impacts is crucial for implementing effective adaptation and mitigation strategies to protect vulnerable populations.

Understanding the health impacts of climate change in Africa in all its complexity is essential for implementing effective strategies and policies to deal with the risks and protect vulnerable populations.

Africa can achieve more sustainable and more resilient health outcomes by investing in sustainable health infrastructure that not only improves health services but also builds resilience against climate impacts.

Initiatives that reduce carbon emissions, such as promoting clean energy, can have immediate health benefits by reducing air pollution. Integrated policies that address both health and climate can lead to more effective solutions. Attracting climate finance to health-focused projects can help close the adaptation gap and enhance resilience.

The ideal would be for Africa to leverage technology for health and climate data to improve response strategies, and empowering local communities with knowledge and resources can foster grassroots resilience.

The problem is this takes money that most African nations simply do not have. Alternatively, African nations could go deeper into debt with the Global North by asking them to finance the technology.

There is another way!

China

China has made giant strides toward its commitment to peak carbon emissions before 2030 and achieve carbon neutrality before 2060.

China's carbon dioxide emissions per unit of GDP decreased by 50.9 per cent in 2021 compared to 2005.

The country has been growing literally greener. China's forest coverage rate reached 25 per cent by 2023, with forest stock exceeding 20 billion cubic meters.

The annual carbon-sink capacity of China's forests and grassland has exceeded 1.2 billion tons of carbon dioxide equivalents, ranking first in the world.

At the same time renewable energy expansion in China continues to set new records, with over 200 million kilowatts of newly installed capacity for renewable energy power generation in the first three quarters of 2024, accounting for more than 80 per cent of total new installed capacity.

In 2023, China accounted for 60 per cent of the new renewable capacity added worldwide, according to World Energy Outlook 2024.

Electricity generated from clean energy accounted for 39.7 per cent of the country's total power generation in 2023, up by around 15 percentage points from 2013, according to a white paper titled China's Energy Transition issued in 2024.

China is also a top player in reducing energy intensity, with 26 per cent down since 2012. Its production and sales of new energy vehicles have topped the world for 10 consecutive years.

China has already been assisting other developing countries in achieving green growth and strengthening their adaptation capacity for climate change.

For instance, under the China-Ethiopia-Sri Lanka Renewable Energy Technology Transfer Project, 11 green energy solutions have been installed covering 12 small and medium-sized demonstration sites and benefiting more than 50,000 people across five provinces in Sri Lanka and four regions in Ethiopia.

These projects are expected to generate at least 70,000 kWh of energy — saving approximately 157,000 tons of greenhouse gas emissions every year.

Some African countries are already working with the Chinese on cleaner energy.

Chinese investments have helped to fund a clean energy station in Mali. The Gouina Hydropower Station in Mali has transformed West Africa's energy landscape since its 2022 launch.

Generating 687 million kWh annually, the hydropower plant provides enough power for 1 million residents across Mali, Senegal and Mauritania, replacing 240,000 tons of coal and reducing carbon emissions by 630,000 tons yearly.

Boasting the world's largest and most complete new-energy industrial chain, China is home to 70 per cent of the photovoltaic components and 60 per cent of wind power equipment worldwide. In 2023 alone, the country's export of wind and photovoltaic products helped reduce carbon emissions by 810 million tons in recipient countries.

From 2016 to 2023, China supported other developing countries with roughly £19 billion in total climate-related funding.

Over the years, China has been active in promoting a fair and more equitable global climate governance system.

Within the framework of the Belt and Road Initiative, China has signed a memorandum of understanding (MoU) with the UN Environment Programme on building a green Belt and Road for 2017–2022, and launched the Initiative for Belt and Road Partnership on Green Development together with 31 countries.

China also formed the Belt and Road Initiative International Green Development Coalition with more than 150 partners from more than 40 countries.

By October 2024, China, an active participant in South-South cooperation, had signed 53 MoUs on South-South cooperation addressing climate change with 42 developing countries, and had implemented nearly 100 projects focused on climate change mitigation and adaptation.

China has also rolled out over 300 capacity-building programmes in climate-related fields and provided training opportunities for over 10,000 participants from more than 120 developing countries.

With climate change and green development listed among its eight key areas, the Global Development Initiative proposed by China has won the support of an increasing number of countries and regions around the world.

It has established more than 30 cooperation platforms, with over 1,100 projects launched, covering all 17 of the United Nations' sustainable development goals.

More African nations need to take advantage of this expertise and turn away from the exploitative relationship it has endured with the rich Western industrialised powers.

These cooperation relationships with China are conducted on a win-win basis. This means that in return for China providing access to the vital technology that will help Africa through the climate emergency, the Chinese can get some of the resources it needs to grow its economy of 1.3 billion people.

'Do not insult a crocodile while your feet are still in the water.'

— *African proverb*

CHAPTER SIX — WORK

'In a political struggle of class against class, organisation of trade unions is the most important weapon.'

— Friedrich Engels

BEFORE I BEGAN my first day of work at age 16 I remember being told by my parents not just to join a union but to become active.

By midweek of my first week in the world of work on a building site I was a union member and by Friday I was the subs collector for the union. My job was to climb ladders and try to convince the workforce to either join or give money to the union.

I was the youngest and the Blackest person on the building site and, to my memory, failed to collect a single penny. It was the least successful role I have ever had in decades as a trade unionist.

To be honest I was never actually convinced that there was a union on the site and I wasn't just being sent around to get abused as the Black kid on site.

I was though spectacularly successful in gathering racist abuse and always reckoned after that experience that I should never be afraid of any union job — least of all trying to persuade workers to support a union.

Years later I reflected on the fact that two migrants from Jamaica — who came to Britain for work — fully understood the importance of trade unionism when many of the people I was talking to clearly had no interest — at least until something happened to them personally.

Many of these migrants to Britain were already clear about the importance and the benefits of collective solidarity. These were lessons experienced first-hand in the countries from which they came.

Whilst there were and always will be individual acts of rebellion the many struggles against enslavement and colonialism were waged — and won or lost — collectively.

Even though the vast majority of people on the planet continue to live in the countries in which they were born there is and always has been migration across borders.

Current estimates suggest there are just less than 300 million international migrants. This equates to around 4 per cent of the world's population.

On the African continent, most migration is from rural to urban settings. This takes place as sustainable rural livelihoods become increasingly difficult to sustain due to factors such as the climate emergency and the wars.

The fact is that we are talking about relatively tiny numbers of international migrants — although you would never guess that from the constant heat generated over the issue.

Across the African continent, migration has always been a way of life.

In common with the later development of migration outside the continent, in Africa took place to follow the seasons, to access water and food and also to escape war.

One big difference after the arrival of Western nations in Africa was that the borders people were crossing were entirely artificial. They were usually drawn up to denote the spheres of influence that these Western powers had carved up between them.

Of course the great civilisations that existed in Africa also had their own areas of influence but it was not the same highly regulated system of migration that was introduced by the Western nations.

People do not choose to leave their homes on a whim. There is always a reason. On the African continent the actions of the Western powers are largely responsible for people choosing to seek a better life and to improve their economic circumstances.

My parents left Jamaica not because they were looking forward to the cold and damp of England and were desperate to leave the sunshine of Jamaica behind.

They left because the British government invited them to come over and help rebuild the country. Or, in other words, come over and do the jobs the white folks did not want to do.

They, like everyone else making the trip across the sacred burial ground where millions of Africans perished on the second leg of the triangular slave trade, understood the bargain.

The bargain was to do the jobs they wanted us to do and we might just make enough money to send back to Jamaica to improve things 'back home.' They also thought that any children they had just might have a better chance of doing something with their lives that they probably would not be able to do in Jamaica.

The same calculation is likely made by many deciding whether to make what is often a hazardous trip towards the richer countries from Africa. But many also feel that they have no choice as the climate emergency bites (see Chapter four) making food and water more scarce as well as the wars — are often caused by the West making it impossible to stay (see Chapter seven).

The migration patterns from Africa during 2024 paint a clear picture of the devastating impact of colonialism.

Libya and Tunisia are acting as migration enforcement agents for the former colonial rulers.

These two countries were the origin of 92 per cent of departures on the Central Mediterranean migration route to Europe.

Libya, since the Western-led overthrow and murder of pan-Africanist leader Colonel Muammar Gaddafi in 2011 has been split between two administrations, each backed by armed groups and foreign governments.

Amid the chaos, the oil-rich country has emerged as a major conduit for people from Africa and the Middle East fleeing wars and poverty and hoping to reach Europe by crossing the Mediterranean Sea.

In 2018 reports emerged that African migrants were being sold in open markets as slaves in Libya.

They were reportedly held in conditions which conjured up images of the slave markets of the brutal transatlantic trade in Africans.

It is as inconceivable to me that this would have taken place under the far-from-perfect regime of Colonel Gaddafi as it is that the West would not have been aware of this trade in human beings.

The International Organisation for Migrations reckons that there are around 1 million migrants in Libya. You can't simply hide one million people.

There is no way that Western nations know nothing about the illegal detention centres in Libya where migrants are kept in virtual starvation and where they face physical and mental torture until they pay their way out or are sold on.

Women and children migrants are separated from the men. There are reports of women being raped by the guards, again, until they can pay for their release or they are sold to traffickers.

I do not believe these depraved acts are not known by the authorities in the European Union as they jealously guard their borders. They know. But for them African lives are cheap and the main thing is the dirty work is being done by other Africans and the migrants are not reaching Europe.

These acts may — to their minds — act as a deterrent to Africans seeking to make the trip to Europe.

The fact is that human trafficking networks have prospered under the Western-promoted lawlessness created by the warring militias fighting for control of territories — of course all supplied by the always ready-to-profit arms manufacturers.

The situation is hardly better in Tunisia — the other agent of Western control of Africa.

Africans migrating northwards towards the Mediterranean Sea can also end up trapped in Tunisia.

Thousands end up living in makeshift camps and often face hostility from the Tunisian authorities as well as locals unwilling to share what for the vast amount of the population are scarce resources.

The drawing of attention to the migrants by the authorities is a handy diversion from the opulence of the Tunisian ruling class.

Temporary camps set up to shelter migrants have faced attacks from the authorities as well as locals.

In one reported incident 500 migrants were forced onto buses in the capital, Tunis, and transported to the Algerian border where they were abandoned. Others were simply expelled to Libya where they faced the prospect of being enslaved.

Living standards for the vast amount of people in Tunisia are plummeting.

The high levels of unemployment that caused the country's 2011 revolution have remained and around 18 per cent of the population lives below the poverty line.

Tunisians themselves are fleeing the continent in the hope of a better life in Europe.

Around 17,000 migrants from Tunisia landed in Italy in 2023. Many of them come from working-class areas of the country and find themselves in competition with migrants from sub-Saharan Africa for scarce resources.

In the city of Sfax, around 150 miles from the capital Tunis, people reportedly attacked migrants with fireworks. People in the farming town of El Amra held protests against migrants who were — in the absence of anywhere else to stay — sheltered on farmland. Farmers said they needed to cultivate the land to feed their own hard-pressed families.

The far-right government of Italy as well as the rest of the EU is desperately trying to push concerns about migration further and further away.

Italy, for example, has reached a deal with non-EU member Albania for it to administer migration applications on its behalf — although this — thankfully — has been slow to actually get going.

Italy's far-right leader, Giorgia Meloni is also working to conclude a deal with Tunisia which she has proclaimed to be part of what is dubbed her Mattei Plan.

This is a partnership with African states on energy transfers in return for them preventing 'irregular' migration.

In March of last year it was reported that the EU was making the equivalent of around £141 million available to Tunis over a three-year period to help limit migration to Europe. Money is seemingly no object when it comes to keeping out African migrants.

There rarely seems to be any over migration from and between the rich nations of the Global North. The exception is the rules put in place to safeguard access to 'Fortress Europe'. But even then there are still processes for spending at least a limited time in Europe.

Worsening security and humanitarian conditions in West, Central and East Africa, forced thousands to make the hazardous journey northwards regardless of the obstacles.

As mentioned earlier, the economic circumstances facing many Africans make the lure of Europe almost too much to resist.

Much of Sub-Saharan Africa is in poverty and, despite the megacities on the continent, many millions still live in underfunded and under-supported rural communities. Many young children are being forced out to work rather than continuing in the education system.

Child Labour

Small children are being forced to dig down into the ground with the most rudimentary tools until they find a seam of precious metal. Once they find that seam they then mine it and bring it to the surface in buckets or sacks.

They do all of this so that the people of the Global North can continue to live in the manner to which we have become accustomed and already rich companies get even richer.

They do all of this if they are lucky enough to survive the collapse of the tiny mine shafts they have constructed. Even if they do survive with their limbs intact they are not deterred from going back to the mine because they have no choice.

These are young children who should be in school but their parents can't afford the fees.

These young children can be found all over the Global South, such as in the Democratic Republic of Congo (DRC) where the blood they shed is used to mine the cobalt that powers our mobile phones, laptops, electric cars, aircraft and, of course, much of the military-industrial complex.

In the DRC 7.6 million children aged 5-17 do not attend school and many are forced to become miners rather than learners. Half of girls within the DRC in the same age group do not go to school thereby being condemned to a life in the mines, the home or the precarious informal economy.

The DRC government has had an official policy of free primary education since 2010 but the reality is somewhat different.

Direct costs, such as registration fees, still remain as do the indirect costs of school materials and uniforms etc. Poor households simply can't afford even these costs on top of their food and fuel.

It might not be the forced labour inflicted on Africans of the past but poor families, whether men, women or children, are being given no choice but to find work wherever they can.

The self-appointed 'masters of the world' from the rich nations are well aware of this but have continued to ruthlessly exploit the natural resources of the Global South in the full knowledge that much of these precious metals are being mined by children.

The ruling elites of the likes of the United States, Britain and France, to name but a few, attempt to us all believe that they have no knowledge that the most despicable form of child labour imaginable is being used to enable them to maintain their wealth and power. All coming whilst the people doing the work get poorer.

The exploitation is not a legacy of colonialism. It is a continuation of colonialism in Africa, Asia, and many Pacific islands. It is also the ongoing exploitation of the Indigenous communities of the US, Canada, Australia and New Zealand.

It is aided and abetted by ruling elites in many of the regions who are propped up with the promise by the US et al of eye-watering levels of wealth at the expense of their own people.

Children, who should be in school or playing the games that children in the Global North play, are mining uranium, cobalt, gold, silver and other precious metals at the same time as the planet is being destroyed by atmospheric, underground, and underwater nuclear testing, and nuclear waste dumping.

India is reported by UNICEF to be the country with the highest number of child labourers but sub-Saharan Africa has the biggest problem overall.

Children of the Global South, as we see in Palestine where thousands of kids have been murdered in plain sight, are treated in the same disposable way that the planet is being treated.

The seemingly never-ending desire to gather the materials needed to feed our lifestyles and to arm deadly nuclear weapons has resulted in the destruction of ecosystems and Indigenous communities being forced off their land.

The only things that matter to the global elite are, as ever, accumulating enormous amounts of wealth and profits and enforcing it with economic or military power.

Indigenous communities across the globe have been exterminated. The Israeli genocide against the Palestinians is nothing new. One of the reasons that so many people in the Global South support the Palestinians is because they recognise it from their first-hand experience.

More than 10,000 children are thought to have been killed in Gaza. It's not a secret. The whole world can see it thanks to the brave journalists who have stayed in the besieged area.

The leaders of the Global North, notably their self-appointed leader the US, know exactly what is happening to the children of Gaza but refuse to intervene to stop the killing.

To them, the children of the Global South are clearly not worth the effort of saving.

They condemn hundreds of millions of children in the Global South to extreme poverty with barely a second thought.

UNICEF says that despite children making up one-third of the global population they represent half of those struggling to survive on less than $2.15 a day (around £1.70).

An estimated 333 million children, the vast majority in the Global South, live in extreme poverty.

Lacking food, sanitation, shelter, health care and education they need to survive by going out to work at an early age to bring enough money through the door to help feed their families.

The world's poorest children are twice as likely to die in their childhoods than wealthier kids.

Obviously for those growing up in the midst of conflict situations, the risks of deprivation and death increase.

Even in the world's richest countries, one in seven children also lives in poverty. Their political leaders would clearly rather wage war against other nations, directly or indirectly, than spend money to beat child poverty.

Only a limited number of Governments have bothered to even make the elimination of child poverty a national priority.

The US, the richest country in the world, has the highest rate of child poverty among the rich nations, at more than 20 per cent, but still chose to spend around $800 billion (around £640 billion) on their military in 2022.

Whilst child poverty is a major crisis in the Global North the children of the Global South face a daily struggle to simply survive in a way that many of us in the richer nations can barely imagine.

Whilst there is no doubt that climate change, natural disasters and war are heavily responsible for the levels of child poverty, the indifference and greed of political leaders in the Global North have also condemned children of the darker nations to a life of struggle and poverty.

As the leaders of the Global North know all too well what the situation is but choose to do nothing the onus falls on activists to build a movement that centres the desperate plight of children, particularly those in the Global South.

Trade Unions

The debate over the nature of trade unionism has raged since the first unions came into existence. There is no doubt that trade unions have made a massive contribution across the continent towards resisting exploitation.

Trade unionism was at the cutting edge of the struggle for African freedom during the 1940s and 50s.

Throughout this period African trade unionism was a battleground between an African strain of Marxism and the anti-communism pushed by the International Confederation of Free Trade Unions (ICFTU) and the American Federation of Labour and Congress of Industrial Organisations (AFL-CIO).

Kenya and South Africa offer two useful examples of how trade unions contributed towards liberation struggles on the continent. It also shows how outside influences attempted to shape the futures of those nations.

Kenya

On December 12, 1963, Kenya gained independence from Britain, after nearly 80 years of brutal British colonial rule.

The early years of the 20th century saw the arrival of large numbers of white colonial settlers and the sale of vast areas of the Highlands to wealthy investors.

Settlement of the inland areas was supported by the construction, from 1895, of a railway line linking Mombasa and Kisumu on the western border with neighbouring British Uganda, although this was resisted by many natives at the time.

This workforce was largely made up of labourers from British India, thousands of whom opted to remain in Kenya when the line was completed, founding a community of Indian East Africans.

In 1920, when the Colony of Kenya was formally established, there were nearly three times as many Indians as there were Europeans settled in Kenya.

After World War I, during which British East Africa was used as a base for operations against German East Africa, Britain annexed the inland areas of the British East Africa Protectorate and declared it a crown colony, establishing The Colony of Kenya in 1920.

Throughout the 1920s and 30s, harsh British rule eroded the rights of the African population and the Kikuyu, Masai and Nandi peoples were driven from their lands or forced into poorly paid labour.

A growing nationalist movement resulted in the emergence of the Kenya African Union in 1946, led by Harry Thuku. But their inability to bring about reform from the colonial authorities led to the emergence of more militant groups.

The Mau Mau

The situation reached a watershed in 1952 with the Mau Mau Uprising. The Mau Mau were a movement of primarily Kikuyu people, also known as the Kenya Land and Freedom Army. They launched a campaign of resistance against the colonial settler regime.

The Mau Mau resistance led the British government in Kenya to declare a State of Emergency following an initial period of denial. The British launched a brutal campaign to subdue the Mau Mau, which mixed military action with widespread detention.

The British response was brutal in the extreme.

Tens of thousands of suspected Mau Mau fighters were detained in wretched labour camps that were overcrowded and lacked basic sanitation.

Detainees were routinely tortured in order to extract confessions and intelligence. A show trial of the group known as the Kapenguria

Six was widely condemned as an attempt to justify the seriousness of events to the British government.

Most notorious was Hola Camp, set aside for those considered to be the most hardcore Mau Mau fighters, where eleven detainees were beaten to death by guards.

The British identified the trade union movement as a particular target for their attacks. Trade unions were (rightly) seen as a significant threat to the settler colonial regime.

Individual opposition to the regime could be handled by instant brutal suppression but it was far more difficult to handle collective resistance.

The trade union movement in Kenya was highly influenced by Marxism with many of its leaders having links to the Soviet Union and, with the high number of Indian workers, inspired by the British being kicked out of India.

The trade union movement in Kenya had been active ever since the building of the railways mentioned earlier.

Some of the first strikes took place on the railways during the early 1900s but the most rapid growth took place between 1948 and 1952.

However, the strikes of the early part of the 20th century demonstrate the determination of workers to fight back against the harsh conditions being imposed under British settler colonialism.

In 1900 rail workers went on strike in Mombasa — initiated by working-class white workers and joined later by African and Indian workers.

African police constables went on strike in 1902.

African workers at the government farm at Mazeras struck in 1908 as did workers engaged in loading trains.

Indian railway workers downed tools in 1908 at Kilindini harbour.

1908 also saw rickshaw pullers take action in Nairobi.

There was a strike of African boat workers in Mombasa in 1912.

State employees of the railway goods shed in Nairobi took strike action in 1912.

Thousands of Africans continually refused to work on the farms of settlers during 1912 during coordinated action.

Exact figures for the number of trade unionists in the country at the time are impossible to come by.

In September 1948 Makhan Singh, the Secretary of the Labour Trade Union of East Africa organised a cost of living and wages conference, the first of its kind ever held in Kenya.

Delegates from around 16 trade unions representing around 10,000 African and Asian workers took part.

Singh was immediately arrested and deported to India even though he had been a legal citizen of Kenya since 1927.

In January 1949 the government and railway administration workers were banned from taking part in political activity or being able to join any political organisation. In a further draconian measure, the British also banned the importing of trade union journals or literature from Europe and other parts of the world.

There is little doubt that a radical approach to trade unionism was critical in developing a collective resistance to the settler colonial regime in Kenya. Whilst this was playing out in Kenya — as we shall see in Chapter Nine on the Diaspora — trade unionism was also a key factor in African liberation struggles across the British Empire.

The Mau Mau uprising remains one of the bloodiest events in modern British history, with a minimum of 20,000 Kenyans killed by the British — some have estimated much more.

The Mau Mau uprising eventually convinced the British that they had no choice but to alter their relations with Kenya. They eventually set the wheels in motion for the transition to independence — albeit in the same sort of limited form it was prepared to go across the rest of its Empire.

The British monarch remained the nation's Head of State until exactly a year later, when Kenya became a republic.

The Prime Minister, and later President, Jomo Kenyatta, was one of the Kapenguria Six who had been arrested, tried and imprisoned by the British on trumped-up charges. He is now largely heralded as the Father of the Nation.

Workers in Kenya Today

During my recent visit to Nairobi, the capital of the East African nation of Kenya, I witnessed two contrasting approaches to trade union membership and organising.

Around 90 per cent of the workforce of Kenya works in the informal economy. The other roughly 10 per cent of workers are mainly in public services and hotels but a large proportion also works in the garment industry.

The informal sector contributes around 40 per cent of the country's Gross Domestic Product (GDP) and is mainly young and women and aged between 18-35.

The government, led by President William Ruto, announced in November that it intends to privatise large swathes of the public sector. Ruto claims to have identified 35 state bodies that, in his words, are 'trapped in government bureaucracy.'

The president, despite all the evidence to the contrary across the world, says the move will boost productivity.

Kenya, according to the country's Treasury, also has a debt of more than $66 billion, which seriously curbs the ability of the government to find the cash to deliver much-needed housing to the 20,000 plus people who live in the streets and the social services Kenyans desperately need.

In 2022, some 18 per cent of the country where humans first emerged from the Rift Valley, barely survived on just $1.90 per day (£1.50).

This means that more than 8.9 million of the country's roughly 51 million population live in extreme poverty.

Over 7.8 million Kenyans in rural areas live on less than $1.90 a day — six times higher than in the urban areas.

Although economists predict that poverty levels will decline by 2025 food insecurity in the country is still a real issue with around 8 million Kenyans (15 per cent of the population) lacking ready access to food. Around 4 per cent of children in Kenya suffer from acute malnutrition.

It is no surprise that workers in Kenya will scramble in any way they can to make sure they and their families have enough to survive on by turning their hands to anything they can.

One example are the metal workers at Ambira Jua Kali in Nairobi who provided an informal one-stop shop to deal with any problems relating to cars.

Back in 2019, a deal was struck by the Amalgamated Union of Kenya Metal Workers (AUKMW) with the Ambira Jua Kali Artisans Association and the Migingo Self-Help Group Association.

The groundbreaking agreement promotes 'a partnering framework for parties in addressing the issues of workers in the informal metal work industry.'

The associations affiliate with the union and allow for representation of these informal workers in legal disputes, conciliation and arbitration and to address the social and economic needs of the workers.

The union also advocates for policy changes to improve the informal economy although, perhaps strangely, not to formalise the work.

At the time Rose Omamo, the visionary general secretary of the AUKMW, and now vice president of the International Trade Union Confederation — Africa, said: 'When we started organising the informal sector — mechanics, spray painters, welders, panel beaters and vehicle body builders — we realised that recruiting individuals was difficult so we decided to work with the artisan associations.'

Instead of individual membership, the associations become affiliates of the AUKMW and their members get the same benefits as other union members.

Unlike formal workers, who can be organised from their factories and workplaces, informal artisans work from different places like their homes, markets and street corners.

When I visited the worksite I met Joshua, who is the legal representative of the workers. Joshua said the 300 workers wanted to link with the AUKMW because 'unions are the voice of the voiceless.'

When English economists Sidney and Beatrice Webb put forward their classic definition of a trade union as 'a continuous association of wage earners for the purpose of maintaining or improving the conditions of their working lives,' they understood that workers join unions to improve their economic conditions.

Here, rather than formally becoming members a group of workers have combined collectively to improve their social and economic standing with the support of a trade union.

I also visited Hela, a garment-making company based in an Export Processing Zones Authority (EPZA) just outside Nairobi that makes garments for major transnational companies such as Calvin Klein and Tommy Hilfiger.

The EPZA is a state-owned company set up in 1990 that provides tax breaks for companies to set up in Kenya and to smooth the way for the export of their goods.

Hela is one of around 32 companies in the zone employing around 2500 workers at a wage in the region of 19,000 Kenyan shillings a month (about £98).

The stewards we met were adamant that there were no problems at the site and that the union and management worked closely together.

It sounded very much like the always doomed-to-failure 'partnership' approach to industrial relations championed by the Trades Union Congress during the 1980s and 90s.

Whether or not the approach is also doomed to failure at Hela remains to be seen but it certainly helps to maintain more reliable employment and a far more reliable source of income than the living hand-to-mouth existence offered through the informal economy in Kenya.

Regardless of the philosophy behind the partnership model of trade unionism at Hela, it should come as no surprise that the union and its members will choose to prioritise an approach that prioritises maintaining stable employment and wages in an environment where a large part of the population is in perpetual survival mode.

But if workers are ever to move beyond mere survival in the Global South, or anywhere else for that matter, they must understand that we are the ones that create the wealth of the world.

Half the workers at Hela were simply disposed of during the Covid pandemic — one whole shift of 2,500 people — with no real prospect of social support from a cash-strapped government.

Hela's profits, as far as I could work out, were not significantly undermined as workers were given the 'opportunity' to work longer and harder to fulfil the order book of the company.

I have no doubt that the likes of CK and Tommy Hilfiger also continued to profit from the massive markup on the garments produced for sale in the Global North.

Meanwhile the workers just look to survive from hand to mouth in a vicious cycle that strong trade unionism must look to break.

Workers in the Global South largely do not have the luxury of engaging in nice academic debates about the nature of their trade unionism. Mostly they just need to find the best way of getting through until tomorrow.

But if we can break the cycle of poverty or millions hoping to pop their heads above the poverty line we must engage in a trade rooted in the actual struggles of people where they are rather than one that assumes the struggles of the working class in the Global North are exactly the same as the Global majority in the south.

South Africa

The contribution of the trade union movement to the defeat of apartheid was immense. I have already outlined much of the background to the apartheid regime in chapter seven so won't repeat it here.

But it is worth briefly amplifying something that I touched on in that chapter — the importance of migrant workers in building the wealth of the apartheid regime.

Particularly from the late 19th century, the colonial settler regime exploited cheap labour to extract gold and minerals. This brought in the capital later used to create the manufacturing industry that transformed South Africa into the continent's strongest economy.

This pool of cheap, precarious and temporary workers in the appalling reserves created to house them was little more than enslaved labour that could be drawn on to work in mines and urban centres.

A broad range of measures were brought in to maintain this demeaning system of migrant workers that could be pushed and pulled to wherever the settler colonial regime needed them at any particular time. It was also important for the regime to prevent the African working class from organising.

To maintain control the regime brought in an internal passport system called the pass laws, succeeded by the influx control laws, that restricted the movement of Africans.

This kept the workers in the reserves but was also used to break up organising efforts. Thousands of strikers and workers' leaders were banned, 'endorsed out' of towns and forcibly deported to reserves.

African workers still managed to build a strong and revolutionary trade union movement.

Trade unions

There had been a number of efforts at the beginning of the 20th century to build trade unionism amongst Africans. Most of these were crushed by the settler colonial regime.

Amongst these were the Industrial and Commercial Workers' Union in the 1920s, the Confederation of Non-European Trade Unions in the 1940s, South African Congress of Trade Unions in the 1950s. But it was really from the 1960s that independent trade unionism amongst Africans flourished again on a massive scale.

The Durban dock strike of 1969 led to national strike action which peaked with the 1973 Natal strikes.

This experience showed the power of organised labour and in 1974–75 Black trade union membership doubled and tripled.

The use of withdrawal of labour or cooperation soon became a potent weapon used during the liberation struggle by Africans in the country.

In 1976, the apartheid regime ordered that Afrikaans must be taught to all children. High school youth in Soweto bravely rose in strikes and protests against this policy and apartheid.

Responding to these actions, workers across Soweto and the wider region took repeated strike action in the first political strikes since the banning of the ANC. Over 1,000 workers and youth were killed in 1976 during the brutal crackdown that followed.

The apartheid regime attempted to make concessions to limit the aspirations of the union movement. In 1979, the regime accepted Africans' legal right to form trade unions.

Between 1979–1983 union membership rose from 70,000 to a massive 300,000. Between 1979 and 1981 there were around 650 days of strike action recorded across the country.

The 1980s were a period of mass struggle that eventually brought down the apartheid regime.

In May 1985, a state of emergency was called by the regime but the workers' movement defied it and formed the Congress of South African Trade Unions (Cosatu).

In 1987, Cosatu held a congress under the slogan 'Socialism means freedom' and it adopted the ANC's Freedom Charter as the political manifesto of the trade union movement.

Cosatu brought together 2 million workers, Black and Coloured, together in the factories and workplaces. With this strength, the masses could ultimately end the apartheid regime.

There was always a huge overlap between the South African trade union movement and the South African Communist Party (SACP). Many union leaders across a range of sectors were members of the Communist Party.

This led to a number of strikes that were jointly organised by the Party and the unions.

In 1946 the Communist Party and the African Mine Workers Union organised the largest strike to take place during the Smuts regime.

The strike in the Witwatersrand saw strikers demanding a wage hike to 10 shillings per day (around 4 times what they were earning).

The strike lasted for four days and brought 11 of the 45 mines on the Witwatersrand to a standstill. More than 500 people were later charged with conspiring to contravene War Measure 45 of 1942, which prohibited Blacks from striking.

Amongst those charged were prominent Communist Party members J.B. Marks, Moses Kotane, Daniel du Plessis, Dr Yusuf Dadoo, Hilda (Watts) Bernstein and Brian Bunting.

Of course the apartheid regime was fully aware of the role being played by Communists and introduced the Suppression of Communism Act in 1950 to ban the Communist Party.

Days before the Act was set to become law the party central committee decided to disband the organisation. The party was attempting to make sure its assets were not being seized by the regime.

It was also a way of trying to safeguard Sam Kahn, who was a member of parliament and Fred Carneson, who was on the Cape Provincial Council.

The apartheid regime responded by amending the act in 1951 to include anyone who had ever been a communist. In May 1952 Kahn and Carneson were removed from their roles.

Whilst it was the people of South Africa that must be credited with bringing down the settler colonial regime there is no doubt that international solidarity also played a major role.

During the 1960s Oliver Tambo, the ANC president, operating in exile, built an underground movement.

He worked with the British Communist Party to recruit sympathetic white people to carry out covert missions deep within the racist regime.

The mission to support the liberation movement in South Africa was captured in the excellent book by Ken Keable, London Recruits and the 2024 film Tambo's London Recruits, directed by Gordon Main.

Keable was himself a London Recruit.

They both tell the story of how ordinary people from Britain became freedom fighters for a country half a world away.

The London Recruits were all white because that's who could get into South Africa without over suspicion by the authorities.

Their activities included the planting of non-lethal 'leaflet bombs' at strategic commuter sites, playing rousing audio messages from struggle leaders and dropping banners from landmark buildings across South Africa's cities.

On several occasions explosive devices, smuggled by the recruits from London, sent thousands of resistance leaflets fluttering into the skies of Cape Town, Johannesburg, Durban, Port Elizabeth and East London.

This came at a time in the liberation when it was vital for the people of South Africa to know that the ANC was alive and well and that the struggle was continuing.

This made a massive contribution to destabilising the apartheid regime and on February 2, 1990, President F.W. de Klerk announced that he had unbanned the ANC, PAC and other liberation organisations.

Speaking towards the end of his State of the Nation address at the opening of South Africa's Parliament, he said: 'The prohibition on the African National Congress, the Pan Africanist Congress, the South African Communist Party and a number of subsidiary organisations is being rescinded.'

de Klerk added: 'I wish to put it plainly that the Government has taken a firm decision to release Mr Mandela unconditionally.

'I am serious about bringing this matter to finality without delay. The Government will take a decision soon on the date of his release. Unfortunately, a further short passage of time is unavoidable.'

The 'short passage of time' turned out to be seven days.

Mandela had initiated contact in 1986 and had held several meetings with Justice Minister Kobie Coetsee and other senior officials.

He met President P.W. Botha on 5 July 1989 and his successor, de Klerk, on December 13, 1989. The meetings were not negotiations but discussions, which would ultimately lead to the multi-party talks that formalised the end of apartheid.

Among Mandela's demands to help create the conditions for such negotiations were: the unbanning of political organisations, the release of political prisoners and the end of the State of Emergency.

By then all seven of his fellow Rivonia Trialists who had been sentenced with him to life imprisonment on 12 June 1964 had been released from prison.

Denis Goldberg, who had been held separately because he was white, was released in February 1985; Govan Mbeki in November 1987; and Walter Sisulu, Ahmed Kathrada, Raymond Mhlaba, Elias Motsoaledi and Andrew Mlangeni in October 1989.

Mandela had pushed for their release as well as the freedom of others such as Matthews Meyiwa and Zakhele Mdlalose of KwaZulu-Natal and the PAC's Jeff Masemola.

The end of apartheid has not solved the material conditions facing millions of South Africans.

The 'official' unemployment rate among Black South Africans is 37.6 per cent. Black Africans remain excluded, with white people holding 65.9 per cent of top management-level posts.

There is a large but precarious Black African middle class but millions of Black South Africans have continued to struggle to survive.

This led to the ANC losing its parliamentary majority during 2024's May general election. It was forced to go into an alliance with the Democratic Alliance (DA) and other smaller parties to form a government , the government of National Unity.

The discontent with the ANC has deepened as the SACP took a historic decision to contest the 2026 local government elections in its own right.

The SACP made it clear that they were opposed to the alliance with the DA and the FFP and accused the ANC of failing to take the steps necessary to reconfigure the alliance that had helped to bring down apartheid.

During his speech to the SACP Congress in December last year, Solly Mapaila, the general secretary of the SACP, accused the ANC of being 'arrogant' in power and added: 'Factionalism, corruption and using politics to corrupt and sully the entire liberation movement has led us to this.'

The ANC has failed to tackle the deep-seated issues that face many working-class South Africans and has developed a reputation that they are enriching themselves whilst millions suffer.

The ANC would do well to remember that it was the working class that brought an end to apartheid, and it will be the working class masses who will spearhead the drive towards a socialist South Africa.

If that requires removing the ANC should they continue to not stand up for the interests of the working class then so be it.

Migrant or Refugee?

Poverty is demonstrably one of the key driving forces behind Africans deciding to make the arduous journey to Europe.

To counter this European nations have created all sorts of rules over who can be allowed to enter Fortress Europe.

Who is counted as an international migrant or refugee and who isn't in one of these categories is one of the key issues for lawmakers in Europe.

For example, people fleeing the war in Ukraine have been termed as evacuees when for all purposes their status is no different to that of Africans fleeing conflict.

The difference is the Europeans have chosen to openly support the Ukrainians. In Africa they make do with financing one side or another but do not want to see an influx of Africans across their border.

In my lifetime I have never heard anyone from the Global South, fleeing persecution called anything other than a migrant or refugee.

This is not about semantics. It leads directly to the way the state will treat you — including your chances of getting into the UK at all.

The whole language around migration is thoroughly racist.

In late October the authoritarian then Home Secretary, Suella Braverman, herself the daughter of parents of Indian origin, was accused of 'whipping-up hate' by characterising small boats crossing the English Channel as an 'invasion'.

Her vicious comments, clearly a populist designed to boost her own standing on the right of the Tory Party and to whip up hatred against certain migrants, have been roundly condemned for what it was.

But her comments also drew support from the likes of erstwhile British racist Nigel Farage.

The obviously out-of-her-depth Home Secretary was commenting on the chaos that surrounded the Manston migrant holding centre in Kent at the time.

The fact that the day before her comments another holding centre in Dover was attacked by a petrol bomb seemed to be neither here nor there to Braverman and her frothing-at-the-mouth allies and friends.

Of course migration is only a concern when it comes from certain countries.

I don't ever remember the same level of seething indignation about migrants coming to the UK from the likes of the US or Australia.

Critics of this comment might point to the attempts to reach this country by what can often only barely be called a vessel.

They steer clear of any discussion over the pure desperation that forces anyone to even contemplate making not just the journey across the Channel between England and France but the entirety of the journey.

People choose to migrate to somewhere new for all sorts of reasons.

It could be war, famine, poverty or even just a desire for the adventure of travelling to and then living somewhere else to make a better life.

The maternal side of my own family, the Tikar people, started out by the banks of the Nile in what is now South Sudan.

I have no idea why they eventually ended up on the grasslands of the border country between what is now Cameroon and Nigeria, but it wouldn't have been an easy decision to make.

Moving from your home to somewhere that you know is highly likely not to give you a warm welcome is not an easy decision to make, much less an easy thing to do.

You move because you either are invited, as the Windrush generation was, or because you have no alternative.

When a local warlord threatens to force you to fight for them your choice is to stay and fight or flee the area.

When your family is struggling to find food, as large areas of Africa are, you move somewhere else so that you don't have to continue just surviving.

I imagine one of the foremost thoughts in the minds of anyone migrating to anywhere is what sort of reception you are likely to receive when you arrive at your destination.

If you have migrated from a war zone then you are likely dealing with the balance of probabilities between the circumstances that you are leaving behind and what may or may not await you.

If your choice is between fighting for a warlord that you have no allegiance to with the possibility of being killed and facing harassment or abuse — but still keeping your life — and maybe — just maybe — being able to build a better life for your family — that seems little choice at all.

The actions of others in helping to ease your passage to your destination or in helping to protect you when you do arrive are of critical importance.

Before I talk about some of this solidarity I want to debunk a myth or two.

I have heard plenty over the years about how the trade union and labour movement in Britain has a proud record of standing up for migrants.

The truth is that this has not always been the case.

Whilst there have been many outstanding activists in the movement who have stood up against the exploitation and racism faced by migrants to this country, not everyone should be included as part of the proud record.

I want to touch on one or two of the less talked about instances of the movement taking a less than helpful or supportive attitude towards migrants to Britain.

After the so-called race riots in Nottingham and Notting Hill in 1958, the Trades Union Congress took the view that rather than racism being the problem that in fact the issue was immigration to the country.

We have been here so many times before and since that approach of the TUC. It goes something like: If only there weren't so many of you over here there wouldn't be a problem.

It's a little like we don't have a problem of racism in our town or workplace because there are no Blacks here!

In their report to the Congress of 1958 the General Council said it was a lack of immigration controls from the Commonwealth that was the problem rather than the commonplace racist attacks that were taking place.

The report said the TUC had suggested to the Tory Minister of Labour:

'That controls adopted by other self-governing Commonwealth countries should be studied and that it would be suitable for Britain to adopt some measures of control over would-be immigrants for whom no job is waiting or is likely to be available.'

The TUC added: 'It was also suggested that a medical examination should be included within these immigration controls.'

In a surprising turnaround it was the Tory minister of Labour, Iain Macleod, who replied he was 'unwilling to contemplate a departure from the traditional readiness of this country to receive citizens of British status.'

Ron Ramdin (1987) said: 'A year later in 1959, the Council was pleased with the 'overwhelming support' it had received from the trade union movement on immigration control.'

Thankfully the position of the trade union movement improved significantly over the years to an understanding that migrants were not the problem but, in fact, racism was.

More and more immigrants from the Commonwealth joining unions and becoming active led to a greater recognition of the importance of campaigning and organising against racial discrimination and for equal rights for migrants.

Significantly, in this shift, was the understanding that merely holding a union card, as many did in the days of the closed shop, was not an automatic ticket to racial awareness or commitment to the struggle for equality.

There are plenty of instances, including the Imperial Typewriters strike in Leicester in 1974, where Black workers were forced to confront union collusion with employers and, to some extent, with the far right, where Black workers have had to self-organise their resistance to discrimination.

The setting up of Black self-organised groups across the trade union movement during the early 1980s, although many existed well before that, was not because migrant workers and their descendants in the UK had loads of time to spare.

They came about because of a dissatisfaction with the levels of support with movement to the racism that was being experienced.

The same can be said of the establishment of the Labour Party Black Sections movement in the early 80s.

The Labour Party had grown very used to receiving support from Black communities across Britain without ever really tackling the desperate conditions that many were living in, much less often standing up against the discrimination being experienced.

Labour had been responsible for three pieces of positive Race Relations laws — in 1965, 1968 and 1974 — but representation of Black people within its structures or as representatives was negligible.

We were not to see Black Members of Parliament representing the Labour Party until 1987 when Diane Abbott, Paul Boateng,

Bernie Grant and Keith Vaz, all supporters of the Black Sections movement, were elected.

Of these, Grant, from Guyana and Vaz, from Aden, were migrants. Abbott and Boateng were British-born.

But whilst the Black Sections movement was often wrongly characterised as a vehicle for careerist Black wannabe politicians, it was an entirely necessary campaign against the often paternalistic racism within Labour and the lack of progress in dealing with a wide range of issues facing Black people in Britain.

Policy progress on migration within trade unions or the Labour Party, however limited, would have been remotely possible without the support, solidarity and collaboration of white comrades.

The sheer numbers to change policy were not there for migrant activists. There simply were not enough of us in the room to make the shifts possible.

Even so, relying on the paternalistic goodwill of those able to get in the room to change policy was never a realistic option for migrant activists.

It was never an acceptable situation to have people talk about and do deals about migrants without them/us being there.

Debates around migration these days are not — literally — black and white.

After the Second World War migration to Britain was seen very much in terms of people of African or Asian descent.

Barely a voice could be heard or a policy paper written that addressed the issue in any other way.

Migrants from 'white countries' did not appear to represent a problem. This betrayed the real issue being about 'visible minorities' rather than about migration per se.

For example, when Poles migrated to Britain after World War II there was barely a voice raised in concern. In fact in 1960 the number of Poles migrating to Britain was roughly the same as those from the Caribbean.

The difference between the two was obviously colour. The colour of your skin mattered then and still does today.

White migrants to Britain have always had options. They could choose to blend into the population over time whilst perhaps still meeting others from their country of origin. But eventually, the more obvious signs of foreignness would disappear.

The option to fade in was largely unavailable to Black migrants although the common refrain from policymakers was about the need for integration.

I am not saying for a moment that white migrants to Britain did not face discrimination. I know that they very often did. I also know that many made common cause with Black migrants to fight racism.

I am also not creating a hierarchy of oppression. That would be futile and extremely insulting.

But the discrimination faced by white-skinned migrants was and is still today of a very different order.

These days migration has now become part of nationalistic debates about Europe and the perceived need to protect the borders of this allegedly overcrowded island.

Many of the migrants the little Englanders objected to were from other parts of Europe but also from places that were not in Africa, the Caribbean or South Asia — but from places such as Afghanistan.

Aside from being invited, the main reason that migrants came to Britain in the 1950s and 60s was because the British had colonised their lands and ripped out most of the natural resources.

The invitation for Africans in the Caribbean to journey to Britain was not even politically contentious. The two main political parties in Britain, the Tories and Labour did so in response to explicit employer pressure to plug the shortage of labour.

Africans in the Caribbean didn't need much persuasion. They were getting poorer in their once-colonised lands whilst the economies of the exploiters continued to get richer.

And there we have a similarity with many present-day migrants.

They are opting to migrate to Britain because this country has been active combatants in conflicts that have helped to displace them from their countries. I will return to this point below.

But just imagine the horrors that could be faced on the journey to somewhere like Britain and the help and support you need on the way.

Of course, there are unscrupulous gangs and individuals who will do their very best to fleece migrants out of every penny they have during what is undoubtedly a dangerous journey.

There are also hazards to avoid that have been put in the way by border authorities along the way.

If you are taking the migration route through Libya, for example, you face the danger of being detained in what could only reasonably be called a concentration camp.

These places, full of migrants intercepted while crossing the Mediterranean Sea, are, according to a 2021 United Nations report are places where detainees are subjected to: 'torture, sexual violence, forced labour, and other exploitation with total impunity'.

The UN report highlights the complicity of European states in the treatment of the migrants who have continued to assist the Libyan coastguard to capture people at sea and see them forcibly returned to Libya.

Back in 2017 the world was shocked to see grainy mobile phone footage of a slave auction taking place in Libya. Human beings were being sold in scenes we thought had been consigned to the history books.

Libyan criminals, who had either captured or received payment for safe passage for the individuals, had decided to sell people for profit.

If you are on the Mediterranean and manage to make it past the smugglers and the coastguards you are still likely to be aboard an overcrowded dinghy or, even worse, some rickety vessel that can barely be described as a boat.

Any kind of mishap could see you in the water and any panic could, and often does, see everyone on board in peril.

There are some amazing organisations out there that dedicate themselves to searching for and rescuing migrants at sea.

SOS Méditerranée is one of these organisations. They have been involved in rescuing migrants, or anyone else, in distress out at sea and to make sure medical help and support are provided — often working alongside Médecins Sans Frontières.

SOS was one of the organisations involved in a standoff with the newly elected fascist Italian government in November. The government of Georgia Meloni were taking a hard line in attempting to ignore international law which compels for a safe port to be provided to anyone rescued from sea.

The captain of one of the rescue vessels, in what amounts to civil disobedience, simply refused to leave port until the Italians disembarked all the migrants on board.

Meloni was eventually forced to perform a huge U-turn and allow this and two other ships to fully disembark while spouting her far-right rhetoric of migration still being a 'problem' that had to be dealt with by all of Europe.

Weeks earlier, another organisation, Sea-Watch, reported that Libyan authorities threatened to shoot missiles at one of their rescue aircraft over international waters as they attempted to save migrants in distress in the sea.

Ultimately the Libyans did not shoot down the craft. They rescued the migrants from the sea before sinking their boat.

The rescue provision by states appears to be minimal. The task of searching and rescuing migrants seems largely to have been outsourced to NGOs.

This prompted a joint call, in August 2022, by SOS, MSF and Sea-Watch, for a European state-led search and rescue maritime service in the Mediterranean to prevent the growing number of deaths of migrants at sea.

Within five summer days in 2022, Geo Barents, a search and rescue ship operated by MSF, and Ocean Viking, a search and rescue ship chartered by SOS in partnership with the International Federation of Red Cross and Red Crescent Societies, rescued sixteen boats in distress.

The week before, the Sea-Watch 3 was also able to rescue five boats in distress at sea with a total of 444 survivors.

Without the presence of these amazing, largely volunteer, civil search and rescue teams, in the central Mediterranean, the children, women and men rescued during these lifesaving operations would have been left to their fate in international waters off Libya.

The approach of European states who have a stake in what happens to migrants in the Mediterranean or, for that matter, in the channel between France and England, is best described as search and capture rather than search and rescue.

A humane approach to migrants seeking refuge seems far from the minds of politicians in most parts of Europe.

They seem more concerned to pander to the basest instincts of their electorates to 'protect their borders' as if these human beings were about to mount a full military operation against them.

That Britain has given responsibility for 'dealing' with migrants to the military rather than the coast guard tells you pretty much everything you need to know about the picture that the Tories are attempting to paint.

These attitudes will not stop migrants from attempting to seek a safe port and to try to better their lives.

The questions for socialists are not just ones of how to make sure that migrants get protected during their hazardous journey or about dealing with the discrimination they face when they arrive — whether from individuals or the State.

These things are really important in their own right but so is having an international perspective and strategy for dealing with the issues that cause people to leave their homes and embark on what they know could be a journey that ends with their death.

This means providing solutions to grinding poverty, the climate emergency, lack of healthcare, and war.

Over the past 40 years China has lifted around 800 million people out of the worst poverty imaginable.

This accounts for more than 75 per cent of poverty reduction on the planet over the period. That is astonishing by any stretch of the imagination yet critics still say socialist solutions have no material impact.

China has also not been in a military confrontation with anyone since the border conflict with Vietnam in 1979.

Contrast this with the US, easily the most warring nation on the planet, who in the twenty-first century alone have officially been involved in military interventions in Afghanistan, Yemen, Iraq, Pakistan, Somalia, the Indian Ocean, Libya, Uganda, and Syria.

The US of course is also heavily engaged in a proxy war, via NATO, in Ukraine.

Civilians flee war zones. On this basis the US is a major factor behind international migration.

The climate emergency is forcing people to move in search of food and water and, sometimes, because their homes and lands have been devastated by hurricanes, flooding or drought.

Scientists are largely in agreement that the rich countries of the Global North are to blame for the carbon emissions that are sending the earth's temperatures to uninhabitable levels and the seas to rise higher at a faster rate than ever before.

These changes to the earth are not accidental. They are caused by rich countries and the greed of the powerful transnational corporations that largely run them. The losers are the Global South who are being hit hardest by the changes.

Throughout history people then move to find food and shelter so inevitably the climate emergency will lead to more migration and, likely to more wars over increasingly scarce natural resources such as water.

The solution to this is not more of the same. The answer is a radical and fundamental shift towards a socialist society that does not aim everything towards the profit motive but, instead, puts people first in more than words.

The search for health care provision for the most basic of illnesses when you need it and not just when you can afford it is another reason for international migration.

People in Africa and elsewhere in the Global South know full well that many of the treatments for illnesses that can kill them and their children are routine in the Global North. It's no surprise that people move for healthcare.

In socialist Cuba, despite the illegal US blockade against the island, there are more than 100,000 doctors and the equivalent number of nurses. On average there are around 9 doctors and 9 nurses per 1,000 inhabitants. Cuba places people first rather than profit. This again shows that a socialist solution to providing healthcare — even under the most difficult circumstances — isn't just some pipe dream — it's actually happening.

The imperialism of nations such as the US and the UK continues to suck the natural resources, wealth and talent out of countries of the Global South. This impoverishes those nations and creates another reason why people see no other option but to seek refuge elsewhere.

Any proper discussion of migration must acknowledge the role of imperialism in years gone by but also the system that still exists today.

But also, in the same way that slavery did, forcing, often, the youngest and most able to leave a country leaves behind a hole that is difficult to fill.

The migration question can not be addressed by technical fixes or laws to restrict the movement of workers. These are doomed to fail.

The only meaningful and logical way to look at migration is to understand that you can't keep just tinkering with the capitalist system. There is no question that capitalism has no future and must be scrapped and replaced with a socialist society.

Exodus

It is far too easy to overblow the level of African migration to Europe. The fact remains, as mentioned earlier, that most migration in the world takes place within borders. But there is little doubt that the continued exodus of Africans from the continent will create a labour shortage on the continent.

Africa already has the youngest population of any continent. Yet it is the youngest and fittest who are looking to leave to improve their life chances and to send money back to their families.

These international remittances are significant for places such as North Africa and are major sources of foreign exchange for several countries in the subregion.

The subregion has a long history of emigration, with large numbers of emigrants living in Europe and the Gulf States.

For example, Saudi Arabia was home to nearly one million Egyptians in 2020.

In 2022, Egypt is estimated to have received more than $28 billion (around £22 billion) in international remittances, making it the seventh largest recipient after India, Mexico, China, the Philippines, France and Pakistan.

Morocco, which ranks among the top 20 recipient countries of international remittances globally, is estimated to have received over $11 billion in 2022 (roughly £9 billion), accounting for 8 per cent of its entire GDP.

The skills shortage in Africa's construction sector is one of a number that are acute.

As far back as 2015/2016 the South African budget made provision for the equivalent of £6.4 billion on infrastructure projects over the following three years.

It seems clear that they knew at the time that they did not have the skills on the ground to deliver such an ambitious programme. All the information I can find points to South Africa not having been able to deliver.

John Matthews, The President of the Master Builder Association of the Western Cape, was blunt in his assessment. He said: 'In the next few years, South Africa is going to be running out of skilled bricklayers, carpenters, plumbers, electricians, plasterers and even painters. This means that soon our limited building industry skills base will disappear.'

It is a problem that extends to other African countries. In Kenya, while for years the capital Nairobi was full of plumbers and painters looking for contracts, today this is less so.

The rising cost of hiring a plumber, mason or painter — who are in short supply — has expanded the share of labour costs to a quarter of total building expenditure in Kenya, with surveyors forecasting a further rise.

Kenya is seeing a drop in skilled construction workers. Only around 30 per cent of construction workers in Kenya are skilled, with around two-thirds mainly semi-skilled and lacking the relevant competencies to be engaged in construction works.

Only around 2 per cent are competent enough, having acquired technical training as Construction Site Supervisors.

A recent survey also indicated that of the skilled construction workers, around 81 per cent got their training on the job rather than through formal technical training.

The largely under-invested education sector across Africa has long been blamed for not providing the necessary vocational training to build the skills necessary to build the economy — especially in the construction industry.

The exodus of African talent to more developed nations is one reason for the skills shortage. For example, there could be as many as 4 million Zimbabweans living outside their country, half of them in South Africa.

The effects of the shortage of skilled labour in the construction industry cannot be ignored. Over the years, concerns have been raised on the quality of the buildings that are being constructed in some of the African countries.

The collapse of buildings in Kenya for instance has been linked to skills problems.

The underdevelopment of Africa by the former colonial powers is one of the primary reasons for the exodus within and outside of Africa.

African leaders must regain control over the immense natural resources it has at its disposal to create the well-paying jobs that will keep workers within their own nations if they so desire.

Ending the vicious cycle of conflict within the continent will also play a decisive role in creating the stability necessary for building economies in Africa.

The next chapter takes a historical and contemporary look at conflicts on the African continent.

'The social (class) relations of capitalism are now outmoded, just as slave and feudal relations became outmoded in their time.'

— *Walter Rodney*

CHAPTER SEVEN — PEACE

'**There is no** flag large enough to cover the shame
of killing innocent people.'

— *Howard Zinn*

IN COMMON WITH MANY OTHERS I was brought up with
stories of a continent in perpetual conflict.

The narrative rarely explained the origins of these conflicts and even
less the role of the Western powers in promoting them.

Africans were largely portrayed as being ungrateful for the
benevolence bestowed on them by the former colonial powers.

In many ways this chapter is the cornerstone of the book. It shows
how the West has promoted and waged war in Africa as a means of
exercising its control and to maintain its control over access to the
rich resources of the continent.

As detrimental as the methods used to maintain control is the viewing
of everything in Africa always as an inferior comparator to Europe.

The result of this is to draw a picture of Africa as a desperate and
backward continent that needs to be saved. It is a picture drawn not
just to allow whites to justify the centuries of humiliation they have
heaped on Africans.

It also draws the same picture for people of African descent. It creates
a major mental obstacle that will need to be overcome if the rebirth
of Africa is to become more than a dream.

In this chapter I want to address some of the current conflicts
plaguing the continent. But before that I want to explore three
examples of western interference that I believe provide clear
examples of how the West has promoted or carried out conflicts to
enable its control over the continent's resources to continue.

The three examples are the Republic of Congo (specifically the
assassination of Patrice Lumumba), the so-called Suez Crisis of 1956
and the toppling of Libyan leader Muammar Gaddafi in 2011.

In all honesty, I was spoilt for choice for which of the many Western-
instigated conflicts to use in this chapter. These three are just

examples of the continual efforts by the former colonial powers and the new self-appointed masters of the universe in Washington DC to extract the rich resources of Africa for the maximum profit for their monopoly capital paymasters.

The Suez Crisis

The Suez crisis is often portrayed as beginning with the decision by Egyptian Prime Minister Gamal Abdel Nasser to nationalise the Suez Canal Company on July 26, 1956.

To accept this as the beginning of the crisis is to ignore geography as well as hundreds of years of colonial conquest.

The Suez Canal Company was initially a French-owned firm set up in 1858 to run the canal with the British taking part ownership in 1875.

The Suez cuts north-south across the Isthmus of Suez in Egypt. The Suez Canal connects the Mediterranean Sea to the Red Sea, making it the shortest maritime route to Asia from Europe. Since the canal's completion in 1869, it has become one of the world's most heavily used and most important shipping lanes.

The Suez is the shortest maritime route from Europe to Asia and therefore a vital cog in the wheels of capitalist maximisation of profit.

Prior to its construction, ships heading toward Asia had to take the route around the Cape of Good Hope at the southern tip of Africa.

Nasser's decision to nationalise the Suez Canal Company was sparked by a refusal by the United States and Britain to provide Egypt with desperately needed economic aid.

But it was much more than that.

For Nasser, taking control of the Company was not only about aid. It was also a demonstration of Egyptian independence from Western rule.

The profits from the canal that went northwards would now be kept in Egypt.

The British and French threatened to use force to force Nasser to restore their control of the canal company.

During a three-month stand-off, US President Dwight D. Eisenhower feared that an Anglo-French military strike would spawn anti-Western nationalism across the region and give the Soviet Union an opportunity for political gain.

By late October, all efforts at diplomacy had proved fruitless, and the preparations for war by the British and French were now in place.

Britain and France had used the time to secretly collude with Israel to launch a tripartite attack on Egypt.

Under the plan, Israel would invade the Sinai Peninsula, while Britain and France would issue ultimatums ordering Egyptian and Israeli troops to withdraw from the Suez Canal Zone.

When Nasser rejected the ultimatums, the European powers would use this as a pretext to occupy the Canal Zone and oust Nasser.

So Israel invaded the Sinai on October 29. Within days, Israeli forces approached the Suez Canal and the European powers issued the contrived ultimatums and launched air strikes against Egypt.

After the outbreak of fighting the US administration of Dwight D. Eisenhower was moved to impose sanctions on the colluding powers and secured a UN ceasefire resolution. The US president even organised a United Nations Emergency Force (UNEF) for the area.

But British and French paratroopers had already landed along the Suez Canal (on November 5) and Soviet leaders threatened to intervene in the fighting and to retaliate against London and Paris with weapons of mass destruction.

Intelligence reports that Soviet forces were being made ready in Syria for intervention in Egypt reportedly alarmed US officials.

Eisenhower reportedly ordered the Pentagon to prepare for a world war and applied political and financial pressures on the belligerents to accept a ceasefire deal.

A ceasefire took effect on November 7, a UN ceasefire deal that took effect the next day, and he endorsed efforts by UN officials urgently to deploy UNEF to Egypt. Once the ceasefire took effect tensions gradually eased. UNEF soldiers arrived in Egypt on November 15 and were positioned between the warring parties.

British and French forces departed Egypt in December, and Israeli forces withdrew from the Sinai in March 1957. UNEF troops remained in Egypt as a buffer against Egyptian-Israeli hostilities until Nasser ordered them to leave in May 1967.

The Suez Crisis had a profound impact on the balance of power in the Middle East and led to the resignation of British Prime Minister Sir Anthony Eden in January 1957.

Nasser, by contrast, not only survived the ordeal but secured a new level of prestige among Arab peoples as a leader who had defied European empires and survived a military invasion by Israel.

The region's remaining pro-Western regimes seemed vulnerable to Nasserist uprisings.

Although Nasser showed no immediate inclination to fall under the orbit of the Soviet Union, the US feared that the Soviet threats against the European allies had improved Moscow's image among Arab peoples.

The Suez Crisis instigated a new level of US interference in the Middle East as European influence began to decline.

In early 1957 the US declared another one of its famous 'doctrines'. This time, the Eisenhower Doctrine pledged to distribute economic and military aid and, if necessary, use military force to contain communism in the Middle East.

Under this doctrine the US began to dish out tens of millions of dollars in economic and military aid to client regimes in Turkey, Iran, Iraq, Pakistan, Saudi Arabia, Lebanon and Libya.

The doctrine guided US policy toward political crises in Jordan, Syria, and Lebanon in 1957 and it provided the foundation for US military intervention in Lebanon in 1958. All while managing to create the illusion that Egypt was not actually an African nation — and one of its great civilisations — but this new nebulous creation called the Middle East.

By undermining traditional British-French hegemony Nasser had drawn the US into taking a more direct and open involvement in the region. Not just because the US seemed to be working under the belief that the British and French had operated without the full permission of the White House.

It was also about the real potential the conflict could have had in sparking a nuclear conflict between the US and the USSR.

But it also was about how the conflict could undermine the profits of US monopoly capital.

Certainly the US would not allow the USSR to increase its influence in the region but it could also not allow any threat to its access to vital resources such as oil and the cheap labour necessary for the building of its wealth.

Suez was a classic case of who runs the world, why and how. Access to the Suez Canal is vital for monopoly capital. Any blockages to its unfettered access — as we have seen in recent times by the Houthi-led government in Yemen in solidarity against the genocide inflicted on the Palestinians by the Israelis — will continue to be met by Western force.

Republic of Congo

The rapid decolonisation of Africa after World War II was a massive cause of destabilisation for the Western powers as much as it was a cause for celebration across the continent.

In March 1957, Ghana (formerly the Gold Coast) became the first sub-Saharan African country to gain its independence from Britain.

With the exception of Southern Rhodesia, Britain's remaining colonies in Africa were all granted independence by 1968. But France, Belgium and Portugal each saw almost the entirety of their African 'possessions' lost.

At no point were they given up by benevolence. It was always through a struggle at some level or another.

One of the first battlegrounds was the Democratic Republic of Congo (formerly Zaire), which had been a Belgian territory — or rather the personal property of its King Leopold — since 1885.

Life for the indigenous Congolese under Belgian rule was harsh, with many dying from torture, poverty, sickness and hazardous working conditions. Resistance to Belgian rule began during the 1950s with a central role played by the Mouvement National Congolais (MNC).

Established in 1956, the MNC sought to unite the Congolese across tribal lines with the aim of creating a unitary and centralised Congolese nation.

Its leader was Patrice Lumumba, who soon established the MNC as the most dominant party in the Belgian Congo.

After a prolonged struggle against the Belgians Congo achieved independence in 1960 with Lumumba being elected as the country's first prime minister of the Republic of Congo-Leopoldville.

What followed next was a case study of how the Western powers — but mostly the US, exercise their power across Africa.

Within days of coming to power, a mutiny of the army was instigated, Belgian forces had intervened without permission, a province had seceded, and the UN had sent in a massive peacekeeping operation.

This obviously created utter chaos for the country's new prime minister who sought help from wherever he thought he might get it — including both the Soviet Union and the US.

Lumumba arranged a visit to Washington just days after the US National Security Council had been lied to by the CIA Director Allen Dulles that Lumumba had been 'bought by the Communists' and was 'a Castro or worse.'

Obviously Lumumba did not know about this exchange and went to Washington in the hope that he could win the trust of US President Dwight D. Eisenhower.

He even announced beforehand that he wanted to thank the people of the US for their 'continued efforts to bring about progress in Africa.'

It's worth saying at this point that Lumumba was never a socialist or a communist. He was an African nationalist who had defeated the brutal Belgian regime to win independence for his country.

At least he thought he had defeated the Belgians!

The writing was on the wall when after arriving Lumumba was told that Eisenhower would be unable to welcome the prime minister.

Eisenhower had scheduled trips to Chicago, for the Republican National Convention, and to Denver, to visit his dying mother-in-law. State visits were usually organised months in advance and the result of an official invitation, but Lumumba's visit was all very last minute.

Even though it was a last-minute visit this could be interpreted as nothing other than a snub for Lumumba. But why?

As I said earlier Lumumba was being dismissed as a communist. But Belgium, still smarting from the loss of its lucrative colony and fed up with Lumumba, was a member of the NATO military alliance.

The US had never had to choose between European colonial powers and newly independent African states. Inevitably they chose the easy route — the path most cordial to its interests. There was no contest — it supported Belgium.

The insulting reception for Lumumba and his delegation reduced them to sightseeing tourists and shoppers.

But the centrepiece of Lumumba's trip to DC was a meeting at the State Department with Cold War warrior US Secretary of State Christian Herter.

During the meeting, Lumumba pointed out that the Belgians had emptied the coffers before handing back the country to the Africans. His government did not even have enough money to pay public service workers.

He asked the US for a loan to be able to meet its commitments. The request was ignored by Herter and requests to meet President Eisenhower or Vice President Richard Nixon were all brushed aside.

The US had no intention of treating Lumumba with any kind of respect that his position entitled him to. To them not only was he a communist — he was also an African communist.

By this time Eisenhower was nearing the end of his second term and had survived Cold War crises in Cuba, Korea, Hungary and the Suez (as we saw earlier).

In common with much of the Western world, Eisenhower was not a supporter of the waning influence that came with decolonisation.

His lack of concern for African rights played out domestically as he dragged his feet on meeting any of the demands of the newly energised civil rights movement led by Dr Martin Luther King Jr.

At the August 18 National Security Council meeting the item for discussion was Africa. As so often in the past the continent of Africa was again to be subjected to Eurocentric consideration with no recourse to any Africans.

This time Congo was the main point of consideration.

The meeting heard from Maurice Stans, the director of the Bureau of the Budget, who later was to become embroiled in the Watergate scandal. Stans had a Belgian-born father and so was called on as an 'expert' to brief the president.

Stans argued that independence had come to Africa 50 years too soon and that Lumumba's goal was to drive all whites out of Congo and seize all of their property.

Director of the CIA Allen Dulles accused Lumumba of being on the payroll of the USSR.

This meeting sealed the fate of Lumumba. Notes from the meeting record the rage of Eisenhower and the fact that he ordered the assassination of Lumumba. To him, Lumumba's existence was contrary to the interests of the US.

The only written record of the order that appears to survive comes from the notes of Gerard Smith, the State Department's director of policy planning. It is an admittedly inconclusive piece of evidence: In the margins of his legal pad, he wrote 'Lumumba' and, besides that, a bold X.

Whether Eisenhower had given the order would be the subject of debate for many decades but it seems clear from the evidence that the order was given and that the only issue was how to carry out the order and maintain enough plausible deniability for the US.

The CIA got to work to develop a plot to poison Lumumba's food or toothpaste, and the man who delivered it to the station chief in Congo noted that the order had come from the very top of the US government.

The US was manic in its fear that Lumumba was gravitating towards the USSR.

Having received no assistance from the US or the UN and negligible support from other African nations the writing was on the wall for Lumumba and Congo.

Accusations were ramped up against Lumumba — no doubt organised by the intelligence services of the Western powers. Lumumba was accused of ethnic violence, rapes, mass torturing and massacres against his opponents.

Lumumba was committed to keeping the nation united; hence, secessionist efforts from the State of Katanga and other regions in the country were met with decisive action from Lumumba.

He insisted on having a unitary government while his opponents in Katanga and other regions, with encouragement from the former colonial power Belgium, called for a federal type of government.

UN peacekeeping forces took orders from the Western powers and insisted that they had no mandate to help the Congolese in the fight against the secessionists. The Lumumba government was left on its own to fend off the State of Katanga.

During the chaos that ensued Mobutu Sese Seko, the Chief of staff in the army seized the opportunity to stage a coup.

On September 14, Mobuto made a radio announcement removing Lumumba and the country's president, Joseph Kasavubu, from office. He also ordered the suspension of the country's parliament.

On December 1, 1960 a convoy carrying Lumumba's convoy was intercepted in Lodi as it made its way to Deputy Prime Minister Antoine Gizenga in Stanleyville.

The coming weeks saw Lumumba imprisoned under extremely poor conditions. In the end, the US got their wish when an order was issued by Katangees top leaders, in collaboration with Mobutu, to execute Lumumba.

On January 17, 1961, Lumumba and his two other associates were tied to a post, blindfolded, and then killed one after the other. The firing squad that killed the former premier was under the supervision of Belgian officers in Katanga.

The official communiqué about Lumumba's death falsely reported he had been killed by an angry mob of villagers after escaping from prison and threatening the inhabitants.

The US and its allies continued to support Mobutu, who ruled the country until his death in 1997.

It was clear that the assassination of Lumumba was planned and carried out by Western intelligence and spearheaded, despite their initial protestations, by the Belgians. In 1975 the US Senate found that the CIA had conspired to kill Lumumba, but were not directly involved in the murder.

Enough evidence has since emerged to show that whilst the Western powers rejoiced over the death of Lumumba it was clearly the Belgians whose hands were on the trigger.

An investigation by Belgian authorities concluded in 2001 that whilst they could find no direct evidence of orders by the Belgian government to murder Lumumba they said the execution was carried out by a firing squad led by a Belgian Captain.

They clearly were not looking in the right places for the evidence or chose to turn a blind eye. The book *The Assassination of Lumumba* (1999) by Ludo De Witte provides clear evidence to show that the Belgians gave the green light for the murder.

But all the Belgian government would do was issue a formal apology to the Congolese people in February 2002 for its involvement in the events that led to the death of Lumumba.

In the years after his death, Lumumba became a potent and important global symbol of African liberation. Legendary activist Malcolm X even proclaimed Lumumba the greatest Black man who ever walked the African continent.

Lumumba was later proclaimed a martyr and national hero of the Democratic Republic of Congo, with the site of his death designated a place of pilgrimage.

Many have analysed the intervention in Congo in terms of the Cold War.

This is largely because it helps to justify Western intervention in terms of the need to check Soviet expansion.

This though fails to stack up against the available facts.

Close inspection reveals the events in Congo for what it was. It was about exerting indirect control instead of the direct rule of the past.

The evidence appears to show that Moscow was not against extending its influence in Africa. Why should it? The USSR was in the middle of a Cold War with the West. But the fact was it had neither the political will or the resources to do so.

Premier Nikita Khrushchev denounced Western intervention for sure. There was no way he could have avoided doing so and, in any case, would have meant it. It was a propaganda victory for the USSR to be able to call out Western bullying.

The destruction of Congolese nationalism was not just a propaganda gift to the USSR but also a blow to liberation movements across the world and to the cause of Black liberation across the diaspora.

Despite this, the USSR's support for the Congolese appears more superficial and symbolic than anything else. They knew the difference between communism and nationalism and Lumumba, for all his worth, was, as I indicated earlier, no communist.

This is not to diminish the importance of Lumumba. He was a vital symbol across Africa and its diaspora in the ongoing fight for African liberation.

What took place in Egypt, as we have seen, could not be allowed by the Western powers to be repeated in Congo. The Congolese could not be allowed to further weaken the imperialist project.

This is why Lumumba was portrayed as a mortal enemy of the West, coming as it did as 'flag independence' became the preferred option of the West rather than genuine independence.

After the ousting and murder of Lumumba his ideas and his struggle against colonial and not colonial rule and exploitation needed to be erased from the collective memory.

Another Lumumba could never be allowed in Congo.

The colonial response was openly racist. The Congolese prime minister's corpse — or what was left of it — was barely cold when La Libre Belgique, a mouthpiece of the former colonial regime said: 'What it demonstrates, alas, is that African and in certain countries with the same level of development access to democracy is still a murderous affair.'

If Africa was a revolver and the Congo its trigger, to borrow an analogy from Fanon, the assassination of Lumumba was an attempt by the West to destroy the continent's process of decolonisation and any likelihood of it moving closer to the Soviet Union.

Libya

I do not begin my consideration of the role of Colonel Muammar Gaddafi as an adversary. I find it difficult to recall any leader who has my uncritical support. But, as with any other leader, I am able to take a wider view about what they were trying to achieve and how they disrupted the hegemony of the former colonial powers.

Colonel Gaddafi was a champion of Pan-Africanism and a supporter of liberation struggles across the globe. For that he must be recognised and thanked.

Gaddafi came to power through a military coup in 1969. He was the Revolutionary Chairman of the Libyan Arab Republic from that time up to 1977. After that, he became the 'Brotherly Leader' of the Great Socialist People's Libyan Arab Jamahiriya.

Gaddafi was an Arab nationalist and later developed his own 'Third International Theory', guided by the spirit of Pan-Africanism.

Before he came to power Libya was the world's poorest country in 1951.

After he came to power Gaddafi made it Africa's most developed country with $150 billion (£116 billion) in foreign reserves and zero debt.

Libya also had one of the world's strongest currencies and Libyans had interest-free loans.

Under Gaddafi's Libya electricity and water were free, unemployed youths received a stipend from the government and every family that needed it received breakfast every morning from the government for free.

On February 15, 2011, protests against repression and food shortages began in Benghazi. Two days later, Libya had its 'day of rage'; a wave of protests erupted in cities around the country which was met with force from the Libyan authorities.

But the protests continued, escalating into a full-scale insurgency, now known as the First Libyan Civil War.

On March 17, the UN gave the go-ahead for NATO and its regional allies in the Gulf Cooperation Council (GCC) to impose a no-fly zone over Libya.

The resolution authorised an arms embargo on belligerent forces and the freezing of all Libyan authority's assets. The intervention forces consisted mainly of French, US, British, and Qatari forces.

It soon became clear that the Western intervention was primarily concerned with regime change in Libya.

The airstrikes all seemed to disregard the directive to keep civilians safe, as they carried out attacks that often intentionally harmed Gaddafi loyalists.

It later became clear that Britain, Italy, France, Jordan, Qatar, and the UAE all sent special forces into the region in direct contravention of the UN resolution.

Qatari special forces, many of which received secret training from the French, later admitted to having led much of the rebellion, advising and planning key battles in the fight against Gaddafi.

Despite NATO and GCC's blatant disregard of the UN resolution, the international community continued to support the intervention claiming it as a humanitarian mission despite the evidence to the contrary.

After evading the allied onslaught for many months, Gaddafi was eventually found in a drainpipe by a rebel group. After his capture he was brutally killed before being buried in the desert in October 2011.

The West was far keener to assist in the Libyan uprising than any other country during the Arab Spring. To understand the reason for this we need to examine Gaddafi's relationship with foreign powers throughout his time in power.

The bottom line is the Western powers wanted access to Libya's vast oil reserves, but Gaddafi's nationalist and protectionist stance made this impossible.

The West also objected to Gaddafi's pan-Africanist ambitions.

In speeches, Gaddafi often outlined his plan to create a new united Africa with its own currency, an army to defend the continent, and a single passport.

He wanted to introduce a gold dinar to back African currencies, thus freeing them from the dollar standard.

Gaddafi also longed to protect Africa's natural resources from what he referred to as Western 'looters'.

Gaddafi once described the African Union as a failure and vowed to press ahead with plans for a single African government.

Speaking in Guinea's capital, Conakry in 2007, Gaddafi said there was no future for individual African nation-states.

He urged leaders to decide to create a United States of Africa.

He told tens of thousands at a rally in Conakry that it was time to move on the idea. He said: 'Let those who are hesitating, get out of our way.

'For 40 years all the summits have failed. Our micro-states have no future.'

This alone would have raised alarm bells across the Western powers especially after Gaddafi had initially opened up Libyan oil markets to the West during the early 2000s, which led to a thawing of relations.

The Libyan leader was soon being welcomed by Western leaders and was even targeted as a 'priority market' for European arms companies.

In 2009 alone, these purveyors of death sold an estimated $500 million (around £395 million) in arms to Libya.

A letter to the Libyan leader from the then British prime minister Tony Blair was uncovered in 2011, fondly signed 'Best Wishes Yours Ever, Tony.'

In the same year, Colonel Gaddafi allegedly financed the French presidential campaign of Nicholas Sarkozy to the tune of around €50 million (around £41 million).

The 'love in' was short-lived after the Libyan leader threatened to renationalise Libyan oil in 2009 while giving a video conference lecture at Washington's Georgetown University.

Libya also made oil concessions and deals with Russia and China. Finally, in early February 2011, weeks before the uprising, the regime announced it would officially divest from British and American oil deals.

All of this led Western powers to decide it was time to remove Gaddafi from power and secure unfettered access to Libyan oil.

The Arab Spring and following rebellion came at an opportune time for the West to oust Gaddafi. The US-led NATO military alliance, along with its regional allies, used its military, political, and economic influence to remove Gaddafi and to have him killed.

NATO attempted at first to claim that its intervention was purely on humanitarian grounds. The reality was of course very different.

Western intelligence was behind the funding of remarkably well-equipped 'rebel' forces in Libya.

The rebellion began with poorly trained young men taking leave from office jobs to drive pick-up trucks, mounted with jerry-rigged heavy weapons. But with time and foreign training, the rebels became a reasonably effective military force.

The National Transitional Council (NTC), the umbrella group for rebel fighters led by defectors from Gaddafi's government, gained recognition in Western and Arab capitals.

NATO, along with its Qatari partners, began bombing Libya on March 19 and helped to coordinate the movements of the fighters it had trained and funded on the ground.

Indeed NATO special forces soldiers were blending in with rebel fighters and appeared not far from the scene when Colonel Gaddafi was eventually violently killed on October 20.

The gruesome and public manner of Gaddafi's death, without a formal trial, was a message that the Western powers allowed to be sent.

The message was this is what will happen to you if you cross the Western powers and threaten our access to your precious oil reserves.

What rarely gets discussed in this story is the role played by other Arab countries in the overthrow and killing of Colonel Gaddafi.

Information is sketchy but it is clear that the Qataris, for one, were heavily involved with the then Chief of the Qatar Defence Staff was open in admitting that hundreds of his troops had been on the ground in Libya.

British sources agree Qatar played a leading role — and accept it actually put more soldiers on the ground than the British.

The complicity of these Arab regimes in choosing the side of the West over a fellow Arab nation comes as no surprise to those of us who understand that class interests took priority.

We see that taking place in the Arab response to the genocide in Gaza where, despite public rhetoric, there has been next to no meaningful action taken to stand next to the Palestinians.

We should also not dismiss the existence of the notion that Libya was an African rather than a fully fledged African nation.

Gaddafi was extremely vocal in advocating for Pan-Africanism. This move to a new kind of politics may have been seen by countries such as Qatar as a direct threat to their dictatorial rule.

Democratic Republic of Congo, and Sudan

The US empire has been directly involved in 107 wars since it gained independence from its own former colonial ruler, Britain, in 1776. They have also, of course, been covertly involved in many more to further their own strategic interests.

If there are lessons to be learned by the left over these tragic facts it certainly includes the need to widen our gaze to the continent of Africa.

What we know about current conflicts in places such as the Democratic Republic of Congo (DRC) and Sudan — to name but two — is that these are not just local difficulties that have sparked more deadly conflicts.

They are part of the quest, directly or by proxy, for full spectrum economic or military dominance by the US or one of the former colonial powers — but only with permission of the US.

But these conflicts go largely under the radar.

Since 1996, fighting in eastern DRC has left around six million human beings dead. Not that you would really know that from the lack of reporting of the conflict or by any efforts to bring about a lasting peace.

The First Congo War, which ran from around 1996 to 1997 came in the wake of the much more documented genocide in Rwanda where Hutu extremists are said to have killed around one million Tutsis and opposition Hutus.

Amidst such slaughter, it is difficult to really say who won. It certainly was not barely able to survive peasants or working classes in either country, but the Rwandan Patriotic Front (RPF) is held to have defeated the Rwandan government.

The Second Congo War broke out in 1998 after the short-lived accommodation between Kigali and Kinshasa fell to pieces as Rwanda invaded the DRC.

The DRC President Laurent Kabila was assassinated in 2001 by his own bodyguards and he was succeeded by his son Joseph who, a year later, ended the war which had amassed a death toll of over three million.

Yes that's right! Three million African lives in just a few short years. Again a story seldom told.

One of the most prominent rebel groups to emerge in the early 2000s was known as the March 23 Movement (M23), made up primarily of ethnic Tutsis.

From around 2012, the M23 group became a clear military force in eastern DRC, and Kinshasa accused Kigali of backing them financially and militarily.

The UN even sent a force in 2013 to support the DRC army in its fight against M23.

Last year, the M23 resurfaced after five years of inactivity and won control of large parts of the North Kivu province by July 2023.

Kinshasa accused Kigali of funding and supporting M23's resurgence.

The DRC, especially the resource-rich eastern region, is home to some of the world's largest reserves of minerals that the Global North has come to rely on, such as cobalt, copper and zinc for mobile phones, computers and components in military hardware.

DRC is home to nearly 7 million people who have been internally displaced due to the fighting and extreme poverty — despite the abundance of coveted minerals.

In Sudan, two warring factions have been engaged in deadly fighting since April 15.

More than 10,000 people have been killed and more than 12,000 injured in the fighting between the Sudanese Armed Forces (SAF) and a powerful paramilitary group known as the Rapid Support Forces (RSF).

Around 80 per cent of the entire population of the country has been displaced within Sudan and hundreds of thousands have dispersed to neighbouring Chad, Ethiopia and South Sudan — but not Egypt (the reason for which I explain below).

The conflict is essentially a power struggle between the leaders of the SAF and the RSF who cooperated in running Sudan.

President Omar al-Bashir was ousted after popular protests in 2019 and eventually a Transitional Sovereignty Council (TSC) was set up under the leadership of the SAF commander Abdel Fattah al-Burhan with the head of the RSF, Mohamed Hamdan Dagalo, as his deputy.

After disagreements — manufactured or otherwise over the terms of transition to democratic rule, fighting broke out between the two sides in April.

A number of ceasefires have come and gone during the last eight months during which time the RSF have been accused of genocidal attacks against minorities.

At least 68 villages have been set alight by RSF militias in Darfur. In November the RSF are said to have killed more than 800 people at Ardamata in western Darfur.

The current violence in Darfur is reminiscent of the genocide in the region between 2003 and 2005 which is estimated to have killed around 300,000 people.

Other countries are helping to fuel the conflict in Sudan.

Egypt, Saudi Arabia and the United Arab Emirates, have all played a role in worsening the crisis in Sudan. Each shared a common goal of preventing Sudan from transitioning to a civilian government over the past few years. They have chosen to support the conflict in order to serve their own interests.

Egyptian President Abdel Fattah el-Sisi's Sudan policy was guided by three primary objectives.

First, he sought to bolster military rule in Sudan in order to be able to control and direct it in favour of Egypt's interests.

Secondly, after the TSC broke down, probably with its help, Sisi wanted to make sure that Sudan did not pursue an independent foreign policy that might affect Egypt's interests, particularly concerning the Grand Ethiopian Renaissance Dam on the Nile River.

Thirdly, President Sisi wanted to prevent Sudan from becoming a failed state, which could lead to significant political, economic, and humanitarian challenges for Egypt.

The latter is particularly important for Egypt which faces a severe economic crisis.

The left must draw the lines that show the links between the various conflicts across the globe, few of which are isolated from wider geopolitical considerations.

The fact that the former colonial powers are still involved in providing the arms for these conflicts to take place and extending their geopolitical influence in Africa — especially to access the immense natural resources available on the continent.

Many parts of Africa, including the ones mentioned in this chapter, are vital for building the wealth of the West. They will continue to keep Africa in a state of underdevelopment to continue access to these vital resources.

Sudan

For nearly a year a deadly conflict has been raging in Sudan between the country's military and paramilitary forces.

This, according to the United Nations, has put the African nation on course to become the world's worst hunger crisis.

Readers of this book might be surprised to hear this given the genocide being inflicted on the Palestinians by the Israelis and the famine that has already set in there.

The civil war in Sudan has been going on since the middle of last April but has largely been overshadowed by Russia's invasion of Ukraine for most of that time.

The harsh reality is that on the global stage, some places are far more important than others. Unfortunately, Africa is not one of them to the ruling elites.

Africa is essentially an extraction zone for the West. If it can extract the people for enslavement to help boost their profits then so much the better.

No, I am not talking here about the brutal transatlantic slave trade. I am talking about the slave trade that is still alive and kicking and which helps to keep large parts of the Western world in the manner to which they have become accustomed.

As does the massive mineral resources such as cobalt which the West relies on to power just about every battery-operated item in the world and the uranium that powers nuclear power stations and the weapons that help them enforce their might.

Not to mention the large quantities of gold, silver and other rare metals that help to make the global elite richer but the wealth of which never goes back to support the people of the Mother continent.

The proxy rulers put in place across Africa by the United States and its posse get rich but the working class and peasant communities get poorer by the day and just struggle to survive as the climate emergency caused by the major industrial powers endangers the Global South.

In March, Edem Wosornu, the director of humanitarian operations, told the United Nations Security Council that already one-third of Sudan's population — 18 million people — face acute food insecurity.

She said catastrophic hunger levels could be reached in some areas of the western Darfur region by May — at the time you read this book.

She said that recent estimates showed that a child was dying every two hours in North Darfur from starvation and around 222,000 children could die from malnutrition.

This is tragic and yet most people reading this will not be aware of the severity of the problem facing Sudan's population. It's simply not important enough for most media outlets to spend time reporting.

They might do so if they can get disturbing pictures of starving African children with distended stomachs like they did during the mid-1980s. Who knows? Some pop stars might even be moved to organise another record or concert for their benefit.

The fact is that the global spotlight is now understandably on the Israeli-Hamas war in Gaza and to a lesser extent on the war in Ukraine, but it is rarely on Africa.

There are many initiatives across the African continent aimed at developing more self-sufficiency and dealing with the undoubted challenges facing its working people.

Not least of these are the efforts to build campaigning and political networks to help tackle those despots who have continued to amass great wealth whilst the people of their nations struggle to survive.

As we celebrate International Workers Day we must remember that not all workers are starting from the same economic or political starting points. Also, we must admit that many do not begin from the same starting blocks as workers in much of the Global North.

I am not suggesting for a moment that there are no hardships for workers in the Global North. Far from it.

But the worsening scale of the hardship facing large swathes of Africa and the rest of the Global South is on a different scale.

This means that we must also liberate our own minds in a way that does not merely treat Africans as victims to be pitied but as people who have something to offer to build a new world.

This also means a shift in the colonial mindset that allows far too many in this country to feel more comfortable about showing solidarity with Africans and others thousands of miles away than we often do to tackle the racism under our very noses.

Expressions of international solidarity or even marching against racism are absolutely vital but so is the need to put in place concrete measures to fight racism in the workplace.

It is not an either/or situation. But it is a time for stepping up our decolonisation of both our movement and of our minds.

But, in the end, it is greed that is at the heart of this unprecedented humanitarian crisis in Sudan.

According to the United Nations, Sudan's paramilitary Rapid Support Forces group is using the proceeds from gold mining to fund its devastating war against the country's military.

The UN report from earlier this year is supported by a source from within Sudan.

My source, who cannot be identified because to do so would place their lives in danger, also claims that the United Arab Emirates, a new member of the Brics bloc, has helped supply arms to the RSF in return for getting its hands on the rich gold reserves of the North African nation.

The UAE denies the allegation which was also levelled earlier this year by the UN.

At the time the UAE foreign ministry claimed they were 'not supplying arms and ammunition to any of the warring parties,' and did not take sides in the current conflict.

They said: 'The UAE is firmly committed to implementing UN resolutions and abiding by the UN sanctions regime on Sudan.'

The UAE went on to repeat its calls for de-escalation of the conflict and a permanent ceasefire.

In the last two weeks, at least 123 people are reported to have been killed and around 1000 wounded in El Fasher, the provincial capital of the western Darfur region.

This comes after the deadly conflict, which broke out between Sudan's military and the RSF on April 15 last year, is said to have killed many thousands across the country.

The two warring groups had been allies in ruling the country but turned on each other in a battle for control of the North African nation with, seemingly, a little help from their 'friends'.

But the pursuit of gold by the UAE has fuelled the fighting that has plunged the country into famine and left hundreds of thousands of people displaced.

One of the least asked questions in a conflict completely overshadowed by those in Gaza and Ukraine is where does the money come from in such a poor nation to fuel the fighting.

The RSF seems to have been engaged in a complex web of financing and new military supply lines.

My source tells me that these supply lines have come through eastern Chad, Libya and South Sudan. The UN has also reached a similar conclusion.

The RSF has used this financial web to buy weapons and the support of hard-pressed young men — who have no other means of support — to fight for them.

But the gold trade, which the RSF controlled before the civil war broke out, remains a key source of funding for both sides in the conflict.

This is a story as old as the hills. An outsider turning two factions against each other and reaping the dividends of chaos.

The UN said earlier this year that the 'complex financial networks established by RSF before and during the war enabled it to acquire weapons, pay salaries, fund media campaigns, lobby, and buy the support of other political and armed groups.'

But my well-placed source from within Sudan claims that despite the denials it is common knowledge on the ground that the UAE is actually funding both sides in the conflict.

Gold is smuggled out of Sudan and eventually finds its way to the UAE, from where it is sold on the global gold market.

But it's not just the UAE involved. The Wagner mercenary group is also taking its cut of the gold. The smuggled precious metal has become a crucial revenue stream to fund Wagner operations and contributed towards funding Russia's war with Ukraine.

In Sudan, gold smuggling via the UAE has made the RSF commander, General Mohamed Hamdan Dagalo, one of Sudan's — if not one of Africa's — richest men.

General Dagalo is rumoured to have set up at least 50 shell

companies within and outside Sudan. He is also alleged to have money deposited in banks in the UAE. Whatever happens in the civil war the general is likely to have several healthy nest eggs waiting for him if he is not arrested for the war crimes that have clearly been committed under his command.

I would be amazed if the leader of the military, Abdel Fattah al-Burhan, had not made similar arrangements for himself.

But the role of the UAE is central to the civil war and concerning on a number of levels. They continue a disgraceful tradition of looting the resources of African countries for their own benefit. Something most commonly associated with the former colonial rulers.

We should be clear that the mining of gold in Sudan, and much of the world, is not carried out in the safest of conditions.

Last year 14 workers were killed in a gold mine collapse in northern Sudan. In 2021 some 31 people died when a defunct gold mine collapsed in West Kordofan province.

Sudan is Africa's third-largest producer of gold but ranks as 172nd in the United Nations Human Development Index (out of a total of 191 nations).

The percentage of the Sudanese population below the poverty line is well in excess of 35 per cent.

Sudan is not just about its gold reserves. It is also a leading producer of gum arabic, a water-soluble gum obtained from acacia trees and used in the production of adhesives, candy, and pharmaceuticals.

So Big Pharma also has an interest in the outcome of the civil war and I dare say has been making its presence felt behind the scenes.

The UAE will know the state of the Sudanese economy but seem happy to exploit the workers of the country to enrich themselves.

The UAE gold rush in Sudan took place at a time when they had become a new member of the Brics — Brazil, Russia, India, China and South Africa — nations back in January.

This creates problems for those of us arguing that the Brics block is a welcome antidote to the almost routine exploitation of Africa and the rest of the Global South carried out by the Western powers.

But perhaps it also underlines a key principle expounded by the Brics nations of refusing to interfere in the business of other nations.

It perhaps also underlines how Brics is not the traditional alliance we have become used to — one based on strategic military interests rather than the priority of trade which appears to be its dominant factor.

However, the willingness to not interfere when a country is being funded to essentially fight itself to a standstill is deeply concerning to say the least.

My sources in Sudan tell me that whatever peace talks take place they believe the country is destined to end up divided much like Libya.

Libya has for years been split between rival administrations in the east and the west, each supported by rogue militias and foreign governments. This came about after the US-backed coup to overthrow the country's long-time leader Colonel Moammar Gadhafi in 2011.

We all know that in Libya it is oil rather than gold that has been the sought-after prize.

The prospects for an equally unstable and divided Sudan whilst outside powers exploit its wealth is something that we must all call out and organise to stop this impending disaster.

Of course Sudan is not the only country where gold and other precious metals have stoked the Western-fanned flames of war.

Tens of billions of dollars in gold flows illegally out of Africa each year, a new report says

Billions of dollars in gold are smuggled out of Africa each year and most of it ends up in the United Arab Emirates, where it is refined and sold to customers around the world.

Over £24 billion worth of gold was smuggled out of the continent in 2022, according to a recent report published by SWISSAID, an aid and development group based in Switzerland.

The main destinations for African gold were the United Arab Emirates, Turkey and Switzerland.

The authors of the report said their goal was to make the trade in African gold more transparent and put pressure on industry players to do more to make gold supplies traceable and supply chains more responsible.

The report found that between 32 per cent and 41 per cent of gold produced in Africa was not declared. In 2022, Ghana was the largest gold producer in Africa, followed by Mali and South Africa.

The UAE was by far the main destination for smuggled gold, the report said, with some 405 metric tons of undeclared output from Africa ending up there.

During a 10-year period between 2012–2022, that amounted to around £91 billion. The report said the gap between UAE imports and exports from African countries has widened over the years, meaning that the amount of gold smuggled out of Africa appears to have increased over the past decade.

Switzerland, another main buyer of African gold, imported some 21 metric tons of undeclared gold from Africa in 2022, the report said.

The real figure could be much higher if African gold imported through third countries was taken into consideration, the report said, but once gold is refined, it is virtually impossible to follow its flow to its final destination.

The UN Commodity Trade Statistics Database, which contains detailed import and export statistics, shows that Switzerland is the main buyer of gold from the UAE.

An official within the UAE government's media office said the country has taken significant steps to address concerns about gold smuggling and the risks it poses.

The continued growth of the UAE's gold market reflected the confidence of the international community in its processes, the official said, responding on behalf of the country's press office without providing further identification.

The Swiss government said it was aware of the challenges identifying the origins of gold and that it had introduced measures to prevent illegal flows.

The report compared export data from African countries with import data from non-African countries, along with other calculations, to extrapolate the data.

Among its recommendations, it called on African states to take steps to formalise artisanal and small-scale mining and reinforce border controls.

It also called on non-African states to publish the identity of the countries of origin and the countries of dispatch of imported gold, and to work with authorities to identify illicit gold flows.

> **'Nothing will end war** unless the people themselves refuse to go to war.'
>
> — *Albert Einstein.*

CHAPTER EIGHT — CULTURE

'While it has become "cool" for white folks to hang out with people and express pleasure in Black culture, most white people do not feel that this pleasure should be linked to unlearning racism.'

— bell hooks

THE STORY OF THE final three quarters of the 21st Century will be the phoenix-like rise of Africa.

A key part of this new beginning will be the development of a new pan-Africanist movement to end what is increasingly being labelled as the 500 years of exploitation and humiliation faced by people of African descent.

It will also be an indispensable cog in the machinery that will build a new multilateral world.

Many in Africa are not waiting around for other people to define what that new Pan-Africanism should look like. They are busily getting on with defining it and building it for themselves. But it will include regaining our lost or even forbidden culture as people of African descent.

The problem many of us observing this have is access to real information on our cultural heritage unfiltered by the lens of Western eyes.

We have to identify what is really happening on the continent and to weave our way through the litany of misinformation deliberately spread by parts of the mainstream corporate media at the behest of the ruling class.

Many in Africa have simply decided to move beyond the flag independence that has dogged much of Africa since so-called independence from the brutal colonial rulers that simply continued to rape and pillage Africa for everything they could get out of it.

The self-appointed 'masters of the universe' have made it clear that as Africans flee the poverty and famine caused by their exploiters they would rather see us dying in the Mediterranean Sea or English

Channel rather than make it to the more prosperous nations.

Lines were drawn across maps of the continent by the colonial rulers that divided people of the same languages and cultures.

It means that there are many Africans on the continent who are far more able to speak to other Africans in the languages of the oppressor colonialists rather than their own heritage tongue.

Of course many of us of African descent across the diaspora have no idea what our heritage tongue is because the vast majority of us do not know our ancestral lineage.

Legendary revolutionary leader from Guinea-Bissau, Amílcar Cabral, stressed the importance of the cultural component of imperialism.

He said: 'History teaches us that, in certain circumstances, it is very easy for the foreigner to impose his domination on a people.

'But it also teaches us that, whatever may be the material aspects of this domination, it can be maintained only by the permanent, organised repression of the cultural life of the people concerned.

'For, with a strong indigenous cultural life, foreign domination cannot be sure of its perpetuation. At any moment, depending on internal and external factors determining the evolution of the society in question, cultural resistance (indestructible) may take on new forms (political, economic, armed) in order to contest foreign domination.'

The importance of African culture is far more than being able to dress in dashikis or having the know-how to cook the foods that are popular on the continent.

It is a revolutionary act to rebel against the dominant culture within the belly of the beast as well as the Eurocentric culture pushed on those still within the mother continent.

As Cabral said: 'The value of culture as an element of resistance to foreign domination lies in the fact that culture is the vigorous manifestation on the ideological or idealist plane of the physical and historical reality of the society that is dominated or to be dominated.'

Cabral added: 'Culture is simultaneously the fruit of a people's history and a determinant of history, by the positive or negative influence which it exerts on the evolution of relationships between man and his environment, among men or groups of men within a society, as well as among different societies.'

I do not pretend to be a cultural scholar of any kind but as I get older I do feel instinctively drawn to wanting to know more about my ancestry — who they were, what they did and how they did it?

I know my maternal heritage is to the Tikar people who can be found in what the colonialists labelled as Cameroon. I have yet to discover my paternal heritage.

But I do understand that culture is a complex matter wherever one is in the world and no less so in Africa.

Cabral said that 'from villages to towns, from one ethnic group to another, from one age group to another, from the peasant to the workman or to the Indigenous intellectual who is more or less assimilated, and, as we have said, even from individual to individual within the same social group, the quantitative and qualitative level of culture varies significantly.'

'It is of prime importance for the liberation movement to take these facts into consideration,' he added.

Cabral argues that the struggle for national liberation in Africa is a struggle for survival. I would add that the struggle for Africans anywhere in the world is a struggle for survival.

As the great Audre Lorde said in her poem 'A Litany for Survival', 'we were never meant to survive.'

For it seems to me that most of us were never meant to survive the 500 years of exploitation and humiliation heaped on us as people of African descent.

We were never meant to survive either enslavement or colonialism.

We were certainly never meant to be free from those abhorrent systems of human degradation.

The fact that we won our freedom and have survived this seemingly endless and ferocious attack places a responsibility on those of us born in Africa or who have Africa within us to write a new page in the history of the planet's oldest continent.

The fact that our freedom was won against all the odds places a special responsibility on that of us within the belly of the beast to play our part in building this new multilateral world where Africa can take its rightful place at the table alongside the other great civilisations.

That future is one where we not only reclaim our past — largely hidden from history — but where we chart a new way forward that doesn't simply follow the Eurocentric pathways that are often portrayed as the only way forward.

We can — and will — forge a new Pan-Africanism world without waiting for anyone's permission to do so.

Just as the nations of the Sahel — Niger, Burkina Faso and Mali — are attempting to do. They recognise their common cultural heritage and the way this has been stolen from them by France, the former colonial ruler.

They recognise the need to reinject pride in that cultural heritage by prioritising local languages such as Hausa over the imposed French.

Renaming the streets in these places from French figures to those of African revolutionary heroes is far from being merely cosmetic.

It helps to promote the importance of struggle and the revolutionary spirit required to win. But it also makes a statement about the importance of us as Africans in our own right.

Nowhere in the world will we continue to be thought of — if they think of us at all — as victims or afterthoughts. Our history and culture are to be unapologetically celebrated as we build a new Pan-Africanism to meet the challenges of the 21st Century.

A key part of the culture lost by Africans during the centuries of enslavement was our names and knowledge of exactly where we came from. The ability to name someone or something is a superpower that racists and colonists have thrived on for hundreds of years.

I have often told the story of the way my father somehow became Pete locally when his actual name was Keith. It was because some local white people decided that they had the right and the power to determine what his name would be — Keith being obviously a difficult name to pronounce!

This is a common experience for many in the Asian community where their names are routinely changed to something that is much more palatable to whites who were far too lazy to learn the proper way to pronounce their true names.

One of the reasons that it is so important to accept when we people of colour choose to designate ourselves as 'black' is because it is our choice and not a label thrust upon us.

The fashion for lumping us all together under a myriad of acronyms, such as BAME or BEAM and the like, is deeply insulting and if you do it please stop it immediately.

It is, of course, not the least bit compulsory for everyone 'of colour' to call themselves Black. But it is our right to choose and not something to be foisted on us.

In the United States Malcolm Little, along with others in the Nation of Islam, rejected the name inherited from the slave owners of their ancestors and replaced it with an X to signify the unknown nature of their surname.

Regardless of your views on the NOI, it's a powerful statement of reclaiming your power.

I was born and raised in Walsall, only part of which is in what is known as the Black Country — and luckily I fall into the area making me a fully-fledged Black country boy.

It is not called that name because it is a land kindly set aside for Black people who migrated to the area in large numbers as part of the Windrush generation.

The area, which has no lines drawn for its boundaries — you simply need to know — or some people say — feel it — got its name after a visiting Queen Victoria allegedly peered out from behind the curtains of her coach and seeing the soot-covered buildings, said: 'this is a very black country.'

But she didn't name it — the people chose it!

The names we now attribute to particular African nations are names 'kindly' provided by colonists who had no hesitation whatsoever in drawing lines to preserve their access to precious minerals and, of course, Black Africans to enslave.

The most populous African nation, Nigeria, an area of heavy enslavement in common with the whole of West Africa, was apparently 'gifted' its name on January 8, 1897, courtesy of British journalist Flora Shaw, who was married to a British colonial administrator.

Derived from the Latin word *nigreos*, meaning 'black', the country was named for the Niger River which runs through the country.

More than 250 ethnic tribes live in present-day Nigeria — none of which were consulted by Ms Shaw or her husband over the name attributed to the lines drawn which suddenly constituted a country.

Famously, after the defeat of the apartheid Rhodesian regime in 1980, a country named after the notorious racist Cecil Rhodes, the country was renamed Zimbabwe to assert a new national identity and to distance the country from its colonial past.

The current chapter in the war on the Palestinians being waged by the Israeli settler regime has also thrown into sharp relief how the ability to name a person, country or region gives power to the 'namer' and also how it becomes common parlance even when it has no real meaning.

What is now commonly referred to as the 'Middle East' only started being widely used at the beginning of the last century.

The term was apparently made up by American naval strategist Alfred Thayer Mahan to distinguish the region between Egypt and Singapore.

In reality, of course, there is no such place as the Middle East. It is more accurately West Asia in the same way as India and Pakistan are South Asia.

What is now largely considered to be the Middle East has also previously been labelled by the West as the Near East.

But, as I understand it, a distinction was made between the Balkans and the eastern Mediterranean, which became the Near East and the region around Iran and the Persian Gulf which was largely referred to as the Middle East.

I am not pretending to be some sort of expert geographer but what I do know is that for British colonial administrators, what became known as the Middle East was crucial to the defence of their Empire's 'jewel in the crown' — India.

This meant power had to be exerted over the area. To name it is to own it because control over the region was vital for the British to easily reach the eastern end of the Empire on which the sun apparently never set.

My point in exploring this issue though is to underline the power that naming has in defining who and what you are.

If you lose the power to decide your name you lose access to your history and culture.

I will likely never know the African names of my ancestors, the exact language they spoke, the work they did and the customs they had.

DNA testing can take me so far, and has been extremely helpful in identifying part of my lineage, but there is much that has been lost to me because of enslavement and colonialism.

The arbitrary drawing of lines by some nameless colonial administrator creates a boundary to restrict the movement of an individual unless they had one of those relatively new-fangled things called passports which have only been in common usage since World War I.

Passports were issued to control entry and exit and when peace came in 1918 most countries retained both border controls and passports.

I believe the right to name yourself is the fundamental right of any individual, region or country.

Taking away that right has more to do with power and the protection of resources — human or otherwise — that will enrich the particular colonial project or show of racism.

We should call people or places by their correct names and reject racist given terms.

That's why I believe we should start referring to the Middle East as West Asia (as a descriptive term of the region) or whatever the people actually there wish to be called. But we must reclaim the power to rename ourselves.

One of the most defining characteristics of African culture both on the continent and across the diaspora is the way many white people have absolutely no problem appropriating it.

Many white writers and academics appear to have few problems pontificating about African history through their perceived 'superior' Eurocentric gaze.

Cultural Theft

As well as stealing African bodies from the continent the Western powers also showed no hesitation in stealing our cultural artefacts.

Why wouldn't they? They had, as we saw in chapter three, already stolen African land. As far as they were concerned everything that stood on it became their property to own.

Nearly 120 years ago — not so long really — the sleepy town of Chibok in northern Nigeria, perched atop a hill fought one of the greatest yet, perhaps, least heralded, resistances to British colonialism.

In November 1906, around 170 British soldiers launched what that country's parliament called a 'punitive expedition' against the town.

The British claimed their raid was in response to locals harassing British trading routes in Borno state.

During the ensuing 11-day siege, Chibok resistance fighters shot poisoned arrows at the soldiers from hideouts in the hills.

The Chibok tribe was only subdued after months of action, and only after the British discovered their natural water source and starved them out.

The arrows and spears the Chibok townsmen had used against the British were then collected and sent to London where they remain in storage today.

But curator labels available online about the background of the items at the British Museum — which holds around 73,000 African objects — say nothing about how the spears got there, the town's epic resistance and the starvation tactics used to defeat them.

These arrows are part of the story of how African artefacts were looted from the continent and remain in Western museums.

While many Western curators defend their collections as representative of world art, the reality is that plunder and profit often lay behind these so-called acquisitions.

The excellent book, *What Britain Did to Nigeria* (2021) by historian Max Siollun tells the story of Chibok and the violent colonisation of Nigeria.

The old African proverb comes to mind that 'the tale of the hunt will always be the hunter's tale until the lion learns how to tell its story.'

This is another reason why African culture has been stripped away and hidden from view. A wider understanding of the levels of resistance to enslavement, racism and colonialism would only serve to make Africans understand the collective strength we have at our disposal.

The artefacts stolen from Africa offer a window into that understanding.

The fact is that museums have served as vital tools to help shape racist narratives and to prop up colonialism as well as current-day capitalism.

More than six decades on from the often flag independence won on the continent, African governments are now, rightly, actively seeking the return of stolen artefacts.

The Western colonial powers have — with only a handful of exceptions — refused to do the right thing and return the stolen loot.

They have often said they can't return the often sacred artefacts because they are not able to identify the original owners.

They have also used the racist and patronising excuse that if the items were returned these Africans would not know how to look after them.

Back in 2020, Nigerians formed an independent body — the Legacy Restoration Trust — to manage negotiations with foreign museums.

Nigeria has managed to win agreements with institutions in Britain, the US, Germany and Ireland for the return of African stolen property.

It still seems bizarre to me that the victim of a crime is forced to negotiate for the return of their stolen property.

The Benin Bronzes held in the British Museum in London are a case in point.

In February 1897, Britain sent 1,200 naval soldiers and 5,000 colonial troops to Benin where they spent 10 days massacring local people and burning the ancient city to the ground.

This show of British force was a response to the Benin king's men killing seven officials from an earlier British convoy, including its leader Captain James Phillips. The convoy had demanded control over the region's palm oil and rubber trade.

At the time, Benin kingdom, modern-day Edo state in southern Nigeria, had been a self-sustaining nation surrounded by former civilisations.

Benin City, formed around the 12th century, was documented as one of the first places in the world to have street lighting. The city had 120-feet-wide roads to the oba's palace which were lit at night by metal street lamps — fuelled by palm oil — that stood several feet high.

Its earthwork walls were described by archaeologists as the world's largest before the mechanical age.

While eight British deaths were reported to the House of Parliament, Benin deaths were not counted — what did they matter? They were Africans!

What is clear is that at least 3,000 artefacts were looted from the royal palace and surrounding homes.

Burn marks from the blaze are still clearly visible on some looted artefacts. The bounty was auctioned off in London to private collectors and galleries across the West.

There is evidence of a prior plan to plunder the wealth of Benin.

Captain Phillips had written to Britain's Foreign Office in November 1896 that, 'I would add that I have reason to hope that sufficient ivory may be found in the king's house to pay the expenses in removing the king from his stool,' according to correspondence papers held in Nigeria's National Archives.

The Benin Bronzes, a collection made up of carved ivory, bronze and brass crafted sculptures and plaques, are not mere artworks but provide an invaluable chronicle of the story of Benin.

The artefacts ended up in more than 160 museums globally.

The largest collection — 928 — is at the British Museum where an exhibition took place within months of the kingdom being destroyed.

Berlin's Ethnological Museum holds 516 — the second-largest collection. There are 173 at the Weltmuseum in Vienna, 160 at the Metropolitan Museum of Art (Met) in New York, 160 at Cambridge University's Museum of Archaeology and Anthropology and 105 at Oxford University's Pitt Rivers Museum.

Officials from the British Museum have admitted that 'the devastation and plunder wreaked upon Benin City during the British military expedition in 1897 is fully acknowledged by the Museum and the circumstances around the acquisition of Benin objects explained in gallery panels and on the Museum's website'.

In November 2020, the British Museum announced it would help in archaeological excavations of the royal palace's ruins before a new museum is built on the site.

The Benin Bronzes remain profitable for their owners, with single pieces having fetched more than £3 million at auction houses.

The British government recently adopted a 'retain and explain' stance for state-owned institutions, meaning that monuments and contested objects will be kept but contextualised.

European state-owned institutions require new laws to be able to return their collections. This has been enacted in France and Germany but British institutions are still prevented from doing so by the British Museum Act of 1963 and the National Heritage Act of 1983.

The British government has given no indication of having any plans to amend those laws to enable the return of the stolen goods.

A common refrain from the West was a doubt that Africans could ever have produced the artefacts that they now have in their possession — such was their intricacy and beauty.

German archaeologist Leo Frobenius, who was accused of having stolen a sacred Yoruba Ife head in 1910, argued they were of Greek origin and not African.

He said in his book, *Voice of Africa* (1913): 'I was moved to silent melancholy at the thought that this assembly of degenerate and feeble-minded posterity should be the legitimate guardians of so much loveliness.'

Charles Read, a British Museum curator between 1880 and 1921, had a similar reaction to the Benin Bronzes. 'We were at once astounded at such an unexpected find, and puzzled to account for so highly developed an art among a race so entirely barbarous as were the Bini,' he said.

Ghanaian authorities have also tried to reclaim gold treasures looted by British soldiers from the Asante kingdom, which is also known as Ashanti.

In 1872, Britain expanded its West African territories by purchasing the Dutch Gold Coast but the Asante refused to acknowledge British rule. This led the British to send 2,500 troops in February 1874 to enforce its rule.

The Kumasi royal palace was destroyed and the city ransacked and burned. Anything valuable was looted by the British troops.

Items stolen by British soldiers from the Kumasi royal palace were auctioned off at crown jeweller, Garrard, less than three months after Kumasi's destruction.

Asante leaders were forced to sign a treaty in which they would renounce rights to their lands and pay Britain for the 'privilege' of being ransacked to the tune of 50,000 ounces of gold.

When the Asante leaders could not pay all the gold demanded by the British, their new king Prempeh I petitioned the British to allow more time to pay the sum.

The British rejected the petition and Asante territory was forced to become part of Britain's Empire in 1897 after another military invasion between 1895 and 1896.

Around 514 Asante royal regalia ended up at the British Museum, 19 at the Victoria and Albert (V&A), and 14 at the Wallace Collection. Several other institutions hold Asante loot including New York's Met, the Dallas Museum of Art, Glasgow Museums and the British royal family.

The V&A bought 13 royal artefacts from the Garrard auction with additional buys from soldiers who participated in the looting.

In 1974 the Asante royal family asked the British government to pass legislation that would allow the return of looted treasures. The request was rejected out of hand.

The case was referred to the House of Lords. In response to the suggestion that sacred Ghanaian objects embody the souls of ancestors, one Lords member said, according to parliamentary minutes, 'would it not be possible to keep the booty and return the souls?'

Another Lords member cautioned treading 'warily when it comes to returning booty which we have collected,' as that process could 'turn into a strip-tease' of Britain's museums.

Kenya is demanding the return of more than 2,000 historical artefacts held in Britain. One of these is that of the skull of Nandi chief Koitalel Arap Samoei. He fought against Britain's railway project through his land but in 1905 was shot dead by British colonel Richard Meinertzhagen.

Samoei's body was decapitated and the head was taken back to London.

The skull is still held in Britain although the items he was wearing that were stolen by Meinertzhagen were returned by his son in 2006.

Empty shelves were recently showcased at the Nairobi National Museum to represent more than 32,000 objects taken out of Kenya during the colonial era. The exhibition, called Invisible Inventories, examined how such a profound loss of heritage affects communities.

In 1902, British colonial officials seized the Ngadji, a sacred drum of the Pokomo people of Kenya's Tana River valley.

The drum has been in the British Museum's storage room for more than a century. It has never once been put on public display like many other looted artefacts which have been in storage for centuries since being shipped to Western museums.

The debate about who should be the custodians of African art has heightened in recent times. It has raised uncomfortable truths for the colonisers by resurfacing the crimes of the past from which they still benefit.

There clearly needs to be more action taken by the Western nations to return the goods stolen from the continent.

Across the continent and indeed the diaspora, African voices for a return are getting louder and there are starting to be some successes.

In April 2021, Nigeria received back a stolen Yoruba Ile-Ife head recognised at an airport in Mexico. While the University of Aberdeen has agreed to return a Benin Bronze head.

But the colonists did not just rob the African continent. They were also happy to steal what was not theirs during brutal conquests involving Indigenous and African communities elsewhere.

I saw a brilliant exhibition at the British Museum in 2024 put together by artist Hew Locke.

The main pieces were the Taino sculptures from the island now known as Jamaica.

The sculptures, one of more than 100 objects from Jamaica, stashed in the museum, are two incredible hardwood spirit figures — one of a birdman and the other of Boinayel the Rain Giver.

They were carved by the Taino people — an indigenous people of the island — the birthplace of my parents and an unknown number of my ancestors.

The three-foot-high sculptures were found in a cave in Carpenter's Mountain in the Jamaican parish of Vere, now known as Manchester, in 1792, at the height of the enslavement of Africans.

The British Museum 'came by' the sculptures between 1799 and 1803.

I couldn't help thinking, as I stood in front of the sculptures: Did any of my ancestors ever set eyes on these figures? Did they know any Taino people? How did they communicate if they did given the many languages and cultures on the island?

The truth is that none of my ancestors are likely to have set eyes on a single Taino person as they were completely wiped out by war, famine and previously unknown illnesses after the Spanish did that thing of discovering a group of people who were never lost.

I also wondered whether hiding the sculptures in the cave was a last desperate attempt to keep them out of the hands of the colonisers?

The sculptures are often referred to in a typically Eurocentric manner as 'Jamaica's Elgin Marbles'.

As I have indicated earlier in this chapter, I do think there is something important about claiming your own name. Although I understand the comparison of the two is because they were both stolen and the countries want them back — and the current owner refuses to give up the loot — I think the chance to know our 'real' names is important.

To fully understand our history without a Eurocentric lens is another treasure that has been stolen from us as descendants of enslaved Africans.

But the bottom line is that artefacts stolen by the Western conquest of Africa or across the diaspora need to be returned.

Cultural Appropriation

We can't discuss African culture and not discuss another form of theft — its appropriation.

I am taking cultural appropriation to mean the taking over of creative or artistic forms, themes, or practices by one cultural group from another. This is different from cultural 'appreciation' where an individual or community of people engage in the norms and traditions of another culture, while acknowledging the source.

I accept that the dividing line between the two is perhaps a little blurred at times but it is something that people of African descent do witness and can often distinguish between.

I have often seen it as a person who has Jamaican heritage — particularly in the use of music, language or hairstyles.

This is not to say that white people are somehow forbidden to play or listen to music such as reggae music. But it is more than an art form. It is a form of cultural expression that has arisen from the experience of racism.

Reggae music is also inextricably linked to the Rastafarian religious movement. To miss this misses the point about why it is a music of particular significance to people of African descent — whether on the island of Jamaica or outside.

Rastafarianism dates back to the 1930s and served as a voice of oppression and marginalisation faced by Africans in the face of slavery and colonisation.

During the 70s and 80s, prominent reggae artists of the time, such as Bob Marley and the Wailers sang of freedom, liberation and redemption. In doing so they managed to help spread the Rastafari movement around the world.

Without learning the history of reggae music, it allows for the cycle of appropriation of beautiful culture and powerful movement to continue.

The genre faces Western stereotypes perpetuated against it by listeners of the music that do not take the time to educate themselves. Fans of reggae can show their appreciation of the music by educating themselves about its history and — importantly — acting on the messages of resistance.

Similarly, dreadlocks have a rich and diverse history that spans continents and cultures. They have been worn by various groups throughout history, each with its unique meanings and traditions. Not just by Rastafarians.

Dreadlocks can be traced back to ancient civilisations in Egypt, India, Greece, and Africa. In some cultures, they were associated with spirituality, wisdom, or warrior status.

Although Rastafarians did not 'invent' dreads they do revere locks as an important symbol of their African identity.

There are at least two key controversies surrounding dreadlocks.

Some individuals, often from non-African or non-Indigenous backgrounds, wear dreadlocks without understanding or respecting their cultural significance.

People with dreadlocks have sometimes faced discrimination and bias in educational, professional and social settings. There is often a stereotyping of Dreads as being dirty or unprofessional.

Navigating the controversy surrounding dreadlocks and cultural appropriation involves thoughtful consideration, dialogue, and respect for the culture.

The controversy surrounding cultural appropriation highlights the complexities of cultural exchange and personal expression.

The line between appropriation and appreciation becomes a little clearer when artists make their reputation and/or fortunes on the back of African culture with little or no acknowledgement.

African art experts have long acknowledged that, of all the European masters, Pablo Picasso's life's work straddled the line between influenced by and outright theft.

Picasso himself is alleged to have said: 'Good artists copy, great artists steal.'

In 2006, a Johannesburg gallery hosted the largest exhibition of Picasso's work ever displayed in South Africa.

In the show, the work of the African artists who inspired Picasso was shown next to the great man's work.

It clearly demonstrated that the undisputed great artist would not have achieved such greatness if he had not stolen or re-adapted the work of African artists who will never enjoy the same renown.

It is unquestionable that there was a period during Picasso's career when he was simply painting African artefacts.

Whether Picasso stole African art or was inspired by it is debatable but it is hard to dispute the unreferenced influence Africa had on his work.

Many famous white musicians have achieved superstar status by stealing music first produced and performed by artists of African descent.

One of the weirdest things about the list of African musicians whose songs were stolen without payment is that white artists rarely chose obscure songs. If an African artist had a reasonable hit, white artists would just take the song, record it and perform it as their own.

Elvis Presley technically didn't steal 'Hound Dog' from blues legend Willie Mae 'Big Mama' Thornton as is sometimes suggested.

When Thornton recorded the song in August 1952, the song immediately became a No. 1 hit. On September 9, 1952, Thornton even filed for a copyright application for the song.

Elvis actually stole it from Freddie Bell and the Bellboys, who stole it from Little Esther, who stole it from Thornton—who made the song one of the most recognisable songs in rock 'n roll history. But despite her copyright claim, the song (which is one of the most litigated songs in history) is credited to the white men who paid for the recording session.

All told, Big Mama Thornton earned the equivalent of less than £400 for recording 'Hound Dog'.

I have dwelt on the issue of culture partly because it is just really important and partly because we will probably never, as Africans truly understand just how important it is.

We likely won't understand its importance because we have lost so much of it probably forever.

If Africa and Africans across the globe are to rise again then we will have to do what we have always had to do in adversity. We have survived because we have shown a capability to invent new cultural practices to sustain us in 'Babylon'.

This is not to say that we should not fight like hell to recover what has been taken from us where we can. But our survival through the terrors of enslavement, colonialism and the racism of the West has been possible because we have been able to survive and knit together a series of cultures.

This is how my favourite music Jazz came about.

Jazz — the classical music of the US — was born from the Blues. Blues is the catastrophic legacy of the enslavement of Africans. It gave rise to a musical style born in the African-American communities of the southern US.

The blues evolved over generations to include African musical traditions, gospel church spirituals, and the folk music of white European settlers in the US South.

Musically, the blues employs a four-beat-per-bar structure in a 12-bar 'blues' form and has, directly or indirectly, deeply influenced the vast majority of modern music.

The Blues began in the late nineteenth century in the southern United States, drawing inspiration from African musical traditions brought by enslaved Africans to the plantation colonies of North America.

Enslaved Africans faced bans on many of their musical traditions at the hands of racist white planters, who viewed certain forms of expression (such as drumming) as potential tools of communication and resistance.

They were right! Those forms of communication were vital in helping to develop resistance to enslavement and to forge solidarity amongst the enslaved Africans.

But other forms of expression, such as the tradition of call-and-response work chants, were allowed to remain, as they served the purpose of maintaining productivity amongst the enslaved Africans.

As new generations of slaves were born, plantation work songs, religious 'spirituals,' and white folk music began to fuse.

Traditional African instruments were replaced with banjos, pianos, and guitars, leading to the emergence of regional variations of a musical style that came to be known as Country Blues.

Early jazz music was born from this fusion along with West African and Cuban rhythms.

Originating in New Orleans in the US, it primarily served as a melting pot for the music that ultimately led to the jazz genre.

One of the main reasons it formed there was that enslaved Africans from a wide variety of nations could come together and play music, something that wasn't always permitted in other cities or states.

The Louisiana Territory had a set of rules outlining the treatment of slaves. While many of the requirements were harsh and strict, providing slaves with few rights or freedoms, a few clauses gave slaves some limited rights.

One was that enslaved Africans were barred from working on Sundays or Catholic holidays. As a result, slaves had a day of rest during the week, and many near New Orleans used that time to gather at Congo Square.

It was the required Sundays off that created conditions that weren't present in many other parts of the American south. Through the weekly gatherings, music was a way to find joy and served as the foundation for what eventually became the great music we now know of as jazz.

The improvisation inherent within jazz is characteristic of the African experience across the diaspora which I discuss in the next chapter.

'If imperialist domination has the vital need to practice cultural oppression, national liberation is necessarily an act of culture.'

— *Amílcar Cabral*

CHAPTER NINE — DIASPORA

'**If you want** to go quickly, go alone. If you want
to go far, go together.'

— *African Proverb*

The experience of the African diaspora is a history of resistance to
racism in whatever form it has taken — enslavement, colonialism or
in the so-called post-colonial era.

One of the defining features of these communities of resistance has
been the efforts that Africans have always needed to take to forge a
class unity.

This unity has been used to defy those who have coveted African
cheap labour but would rather we didn't exist in their presence.

Africans in the diaspora have lived the double consciousness that the
great W.E.B. Du bois so brilliantly articulated.

Du bois was, of course, referring to the specific experience of African
Americans — which I do not cover in this chapter as that will form
the core of a later book in this series.

Under the title 'Of Our Spiritual Strivings' in the classic work, *The
Souls of Black Folk*, Du bois said:

'It is a peculiar sensation, this double-consciousness, this sense of
always looking at one's self through the eyes of others, of measuring
one's soul by the tape of a world that looks on in amused contempt
and pity.

'One ever feels his two-ness,—an American, a Negro; two souls, two
thoughts, two unreconciled strivings; two warring ideals in one dark
body, whose dogged strength alone keeps it from being torn asunder.

'The history of the American Negro is the history of this strife —
this longing to attain self-conscious manhood, to merge his double
self into a better and truer self. In this merging he wishes neither of
the older selves to be lost. He does not wish to Africanise America,
for America has too much to teach the world and Africa.

'He wouldn't bleach his Negro blood in a flood of white Americanism,
for he knows that Negro blood has a message for the world.

'He simply wishes to make it possible for a man to be both a Negro and an American without being cursed and spit upon by his fellows, without having the doors of opportunity closed roughly in his face.'

This double consciousness can be applied to anywhere across the African diaspora. But always, wherever we can be found, Africans have found ways of building a unity to resist our oppression.

The Growth of the International Black Power Movement

The early 1960s saw the four largest British territories in the Caribbean and some of the most important in the African diaspora — Jamaica, Trinidad and Tobago, Barbados and British Guiana — all became independent.

It was a time when the nature of African resistance to racism took on a new character as the International Black Power Movement began to take hold.

The nature of independence from Britain should detain us for a few moments because it provides us with one of the key terrains of resistance against racism that was to continue to be fought by Black Power activists.

The reality is that Britain still exercises control in these countries through the Commonwealth and the British Privy Council — which remains the final court of appeal in the country. Essentially independence did not bring about a reordering of society in these countries.

The consequence of this failure to bring about fundamental change was the creation of social movements opposed to the politics of the national elite.

Walter Rodney (1969) argues this point when he asserts 'a Black man ruling a dependent State within the imperialist system has no power. He is simply an agent of the whites in the metropolis, with an army and a police force designed to maintain the imperialist way of things.'

The British even tried to 'modernise' its control over its soon-to-be independent colonies through the creation of a West Indian Federation.

The Federation was born in 1958 and finally died in 1962. The aim was to provide a unified system of government for their colonies and former colonies in the West Indies.

Although the project was plagued by bickering between the islands from the outset, moves to create more political unity between the Island States remain a strong current in the politics of the region.

For much the same reason that the politics of Pan-Africanism is still a strong influence in the area, namely a sense of Black pride and a recognition of the strength achieved through unity, so the idea of a strong unified region remains appealing to some.

The reasons for the demise of the first attempt at forming a Federation are, not surprisingly, somewhat contested. Some believe that the Federation's demise is because of moves towards a federal centre more powerful than the member states.

It could be argued that this led to the withdrawal of the not-yet-independent Jamaica in 1961 (see below).

It could also be argued that the Federation was a project doomed to failure because it was part of the post-colonial project of the British Government designed to maintain power in the region.

The debate on the merits or otherwise of the West Indian Federation ideal is severely hindered by the paucity of writing on the subject.

Even though there are those who, as described above, would see such a move as a progressive means of uniting the former colonial states in the region, precious little has been written to advance the argument by learning from the experience of the past formation of such a body.

However, independence was now firmly in the air both in a nationalistic sense and, with it, a greater sense of Black pride. This new sense of African pride was reflected in the growth of the Black Power Movement.

This period was a particularly radical period in the growth and development of the Black resistance movement in Britain (because from the mid-1960s onwards this was the most appropriate description) and the later formation of communities of resistance in trade unions.

It's very easy to see the African resistance movement across the diaspora as a mere adjunct of the somehow more romantic and seemingly high-profile events taking place in the US.

While there is little doubt as to the important influence that events and leaders from Stateside had on what was to take place across the diaspora it is best characterised as influential rather than defining.

Blacks in the diaspora and the US, while sharing a common legacy of slavery or indentured labour, have a particular history.

This, along with the Canadian experience, will be covered in the final book in the trilogy of 'the three worlds'.

This chapter provides some historical context for the diaspora and foregrounds the resistance to racism that has been a key characteristic of the African presence in the belly of the beast.

It would simply be wrong to begin this discussion anywhere other than Haiti where Africans became — against all the odds — the first enslaved people to overthrow their bondage and create their nation.

Haiti

Haiti is not where the resistance to racism began by any means but it is where the first world-shaking victory against the slavers and the colonists took place.

One of those is the continuing battle for justice over the transatlantic slave trade and its continuing impact on the lives of people of African descent.

Nowhere is this more starkly demonstrated than in Haiti.

In the preface to the first edition of the classic study of the Haitian revolution C.L.R. James describes it best.

'In August 1791, after two years of the French Revolution and its repercussions in San Domingo, the slaves revolted. The struggle lasted for twelve years. The slaves defeated in turn the local whites and the soldiers of the French monarchy, a Spanish invasion, a British expedition of some 60,000 men, and a French expedition of similar size under Bonaparte's brother-in-law. The defeat of Bonaparte's expedition in 1803 resulted in the establishment of the Negro state of Haiti which has lasted to this day.'

Haiti continues to be the victim of international collective punishment for daring to be the world's first African-led republic and the first independent Caribbean state after it threw off the yoke of French colonial rule and slavery in 1824.

This victory came at a crippling cost for Haiti.

The country was forced to pay compensation of 150 million French francs to their former slave owners as part of the cost for their freedom.

This amounted to 30 times Haiti's annual revenue.

Estimates put Haiti's payments at the equivalent of what is now $560 million to France over seven decades with the true economic cost to Haiti put at an astounding $115 billion.

So slave owners who made a fortune from the free labour that produced sugar, indigo, cotton and coffee, made the descendants of those slaves pay them even greater riches while Haiti became the most impoverished nation in the western hemisphere.

These forced repayments contributed greatly to the woes still being experienced in Haiti today.

Haiti was forced to borrow heavily from international banks which, of course, charged extremely high interest rates on the debt.

Although the debt owed was later reduced to 90 million francs in 1838, by 1900 some 80 per cent of Haiti's government spending was on debt repayment.

This scandalous ransom was not fully repaid by the Haitians until 1947.

Not surprisingly there have been many demands for France to repay the money back to Haiti and to make reparations for slavery itself.

In 2004, the Haitian government demanded that the French give back the millions they had paid to the former slave masters.

Not surprisingly, as with most other calls by people of African descent for repayments relating to slavery, the former oppressors have failed to come up with the cash or even any proposals that might remotely start to address the issue.

The disgusting notion that slave owners should be compensated for their 'lost property' is, of course, not new.

The same process took place in Britain when slave owners, and not the enslaved, were paid money.

A then incredible £20 million package for British slave owners was agreed for that very purpose through the Slave Compensation Act of 1837.

Some 40,000 direct payments were paid to British slavers.

Overall Britain's 'slavery debt' was not repaid until as recently as 2015.

But back in Haiti, they have the constant spectre of the US looming large.

As far as the US is concerned Haiti, just under 2,000 miles away, falls within its 'backyard' or its political and military sphere of influence.

The US has continually interfered in the domestic affairs of Haiti and clearly regards it as its right to do so.

Amidst all the current talk of sovereignty relating to Russia's invasion of Ukraine it is worth remembering that in 1915 the US invaded sovereign Haiti because they believed unrest in the country was endangering American financial investments.

US troops stayed in Haiti until 1934 but effectively remained in political and financial control until after World War II, in 1947.

After the overthrow of President Jean-Bertrand Aristide in 1991, US President Bill Clinton sent 20,000 troops back to the island in 1994 to 'restore democracy' or rather control, at the point of a gun.

President Aristide was ousted again in 2004 which led to thousands of US Marines being sent back to the island and the involvement of a so-called United Nations 'stabilisation' force that was only withdrawn in 2017.

The former French ambassador to Haiti, Thierry Burkhard, admitted to the New York Times that France and the US were behind the 2004 ousting of Aristide from power.

Burkhard said that one of the benefits of removing Aristide was putting an end to his campaign demanding that France pay financial reparations to Haiti.

In July 2021, President Jovenel Moise was assassinated in July 2021 by unidentified gunmen in the capital, Port-au-Prince with many on the island suggesting that the US may have been involved — directly or indirectly.

Critics have accused prime minister-designate Ariel Henry of collusion with political allies on the island and the US in the assassination of Moise.

A General Election has been promised for this year but this seems a very remote prospect as the economy has all but collapsed and gangs across the island have moved in to fill the vacuum.

The capital Port-au-Prince is the centre of a horrific turf war in which there have been kidnappings, rape as well as countless civilian deaths.

Gangs have operated in tandem with politicians to intimidate rivals and deliver votes with their activities financed partly through the international drug trade.

It is clear that the economic and political turmoil in the country has made a huge contribution towards the inability of Haiti to withstand the seemingly endless stream of devastating natural disasters that plague the country.

After the 2010 earthquake all but destroyed Haiti, scholars and journalists wrote a letter to the French president, Nicolas Sarkozy, demanding that France pay back Haiti.

Sarkozy, like all French presidents, refused to even engage with the idea.

A collapsed economy, caused, as I have argued, by the West, gang violence or natural disasters are not excuses that should allow for military intervention into Haiti.

Aid and advice are, of course, very welcome. But none of that should be an excuse to further entrench colonial control of Haiti through the usual stringent conditions applied by the World Bank or International Monetary Fund through their structural adjustment packages.

These packages, largely benefiting US transnational corporations, would simply allow the West to wield power over the Haitians in a manner that would be difficult to distinguish from the old-style colonial rule.

We must keep the issue of reparations on the table for Haiti as well as the principle of non-intervention in this sovereign country.

After all, what's good for Ukraine must be good for Haiti.

But if the rich nations of the world want to help right the wrongs done to Haiti in the past by the French, the US and their collaborators, perhaps the most effective policy right now would be to accept more Haitian refugees.

This wouldn't only be a humane policy that would improve their lives and that of their families.

It might also mean expatriates being able to send money back home to Haiti to help stimulate the ailing economy of the country.

Brazil

I have mentioned elsewhere in this book that more enslaved Africans were forcibly transported to Brazil than to any other single destination.

Brazil is largely seen as a party place where everyone enjoys carnival and unites around a common love of football.

Some of the greatest football players of all time have been Brazilians of African descent. Their ancestors were enslaved and survived some of the harshest plantation conditions ever known to humankind.

Prior to the invasion of the Europeans, the lands now known as Brazil were occupied by a diverse group of indigenous tribes.

The Europeans arrived on April 22, 1500 in the shape of Pedro Álvares Cabral who was sponsored by the Portuguese and the Catholic Church. The area was briefly called 'Land of the Holy Cross' by the Portuguese before the name 'Land of Brazil' was given by colonial settlers and merchants who were dealing in brazilwood.

Brazilwood was extremely profitable and particularly valued for its durability, unique colours and suitability for the growing construction and furniture-making industry of the time.

Through the first half of the 16th century there was little Portuguese appetite for occupying Brazil. They were able to make far more profits through trading with India and China.

But after the country began to be raided by foreign nations — including France that established a short-lived colony in 1555 — the Portuguese began to colonise the land to safeguard its profits.

It soon became clear to the Portuguese that maximising profits in the area would be problematic on such a vast territory.

The Portuguese first turned to the enslavement of indigenous people of the area. They were forced to turn their hand to agricultural work and to the expanding sugar industry.

The indigenous enslaved population soon began to dwindle because of harsh treatment as well as the diseases they were being exposed to that the Portuguese had brought with them.

As time went by it became increasingly clear to the Portuguese that indigenous enslavement alone was not going to be sufficient to meet the need of the labour demands of the sugar plantations.

So from 1570 enslaved Africans became increasingly used to work on the lucrative sugar plantations even though indigenous enslavement continued well into the 18th century.

On average enslaved Africans only reached the age of 23. The working conditions and the harsh treatment of the slave owners were simply too harsh.

The conditions endured by the enslaved Africans varied depending on what work they were being forced to do and the region they were in.

For instance, in sugar plantations in the Bahia region, African slaves were treated extremely harshly and fed meagre rations.

They were forced to work hard over long hours because the profit they generated outweighed the profit lost from an enslaved African with a short life span.

In the mountainous mining region of Minas Gerais, while the work was tough, slaves were valued more and allowed some amount of autonomy.

As I have discussed elsewhere in this book, where there was enslavement there was racism and where there was racism there was resistance.

Whilst there were major revolts by enslaved Africans in Brazil — such as in 1798, 1807, 1814 and 1835 — the most common form of resistance to enslavement was the formation of settlements called Quilombos by Africans who had managed to escape.

These settlements were set up mostly in the Bahia and Minas Gerais regions, as well as in the remote frontier region of Alagoas, where the largest and most famous *quilombo*, Palmeres, was established.

But there were also major acts of rebellion against the Portuguese rulers that managed to shake the slavery establishment.

The Revolt of the Buzios took place in 1798 in Bahia.

The revolt was a separatist movement largely inspired by the French Revolution. The leaders were mostly free 'mulattos', but a second group of wealthier whites who encouraged the revolt were not prosecuted.

One of the goals of the rebellion was to liberate the enslaved Africans. Those taking part included freed Africans, enslaved Africans, artisans and tailors.

With many enslaved Africans living in Bahia, the probability of revolts and rebellions ran high. The elites of the area were frightened that if rebellion or revolts did happen, they would be similar to the Haitian Revolution.

Because of the significant participation of Bahia's lower classes, the revolt has also been dubbed 'The First Brazilian Social Revolution'.

In 1807, enslaved Africans were planning a revolt that would take place on May 28, during Corpus Christi celebrations.

But six days before the revolt was due to take place they were betrayed by an enslaved African who chose loyalty to his master.

A day before the rebellion was due to take place the governor had mounted specific patrols in the city. With its exits and entrances under surveillance, and rural officers on the roads, the house that was the centre of the planning was surrounded and searched.

After being searched the alleged leaders and captains were taken prisoner. Three of the ringleaders who had fled earlier that afternoon were soon rounded up.

The goal of the uprising is believed to have been to capture ships in the harbour and to sail back to Africa.

The rebellion of 1814 overshadowed the previous ones in the number of participants and violence. Starting on February 28, enslaved fishermen began to burn down part of the harbour, killing the foreman and most of his family. The rebels then headed to the village of Itapoã.

Resistance was met when they began heading to the next village. Troops from Salvador then slaughtered the rebels — leaving fewer than 50 alive.

Four of the captured slaves were hanged in public and 12 were deported to the equally brutal Portuguese colonies in Africa.

The Muslim Slave revolt in 1835 began January 24, 1835 by rebellion organisers, Malês, or Muslim Africans. The revolt took place in the streets of Salvador and lasted for three hours.

During the revolt, 70 people were slaughtered and afterwards, more than 500 were either sentenced to death, imprisoned, whipped or deported.

The testimonies during the sham court proceeding — where the verdict was already well-known — Africans spoke out about the harsh treatment that they had been subjected to that caused them to mount the rebellion. But the rebels also objected to their enslavement.

Cuba

Cuba has faced vilification from many Western countries for alleged high levels of racism on the Caribbean island. These criticisms have been levelled by nations who have systematically abused, exploited and, in some cases, practised what can only be described as apartheid within their own borders.

I do not claim for a moment that everything in Cuba is perfect. At the time of scribbling these words, I have never had the opportunity to visit Cuba to see for myself.

Neither do I claim that just because the Cubans are attempting to build a socialist society that everything is de-facto perfect. I can only go on the basis of the evidence that I can find.

The United Nations commemorated the end of the International Decade for People of African Descent 2015–2024 with a conference themed 'Equality — Equity — Social Justice'. Over 100 delegates came from 18 countries representing North America, Central America, the Caribbean, South America and Africa.

Delegates, including representatives from international organisations such as the Diaspora Division in the African Union, spent a week in mid-December of 2024 attending plenary sessions, workshops and touring Cuba to learn about the country's work against racism and discrimination.

A group of delegates—including acclaimed actor Danny Glover, Barbadian David Denny, secretary general of the Caribbean Peace Movement and Geoffroy De Laforcade, professor of history at Norfolk State University—were welcomed to the island nation by Miguel Díaz-Canel Bermúdez, President and First Secretary of the Central Committee of the Communist Party.

Despite more than 60 years of a crippling illegal unilateral US embargo against Cuba which has caused hardships for generations of Cubans, the country is clearly actively attempting to combat racism.

In 1959, after a six-year war, the Cuban Revolution led by Fidel Castro overthrew the US-backed dictator Fulgencio Batista.

The revolution profoundly reshaped Cuba's political, social, and economic landscape and had far-reaching implications for the global Cold War era.

Comandante Fidel's revolutionary government nationalised industries, redistributed land, and sought to pursue socialist policies.

The US saw Cuba as a threat to its influence in the Western Hemisphere.

In 1961, the US tried to invade Cuba with the infamous Bay of Pigs Invasion. It was a failed military operation by Cuban exiles, backed by the US, to overthrow the Cuban revolution.

This attempted invasion marked a significant Cold War flashpoint and strained US-Cuban relations, further cementing Cuba's alignment with the then-Soviet Union.

The US responded in 1962 with the longest-running economic sanctions that continue today.

The blockade restricts trade between the US and Cuba, including food and medicine. However, there are exceptions for family visits, educational exchanges, and religious activities.

This illegal action by the US makes it virtually impossible for Cuba to access international banking and financing. The blockade has significantly hindered Cuba's economic development, leading to shortages of essential goods and services.

Since 1992, the United Nations General Assembly has annually endorsed a resolution calling for the termination of the blockade.

The US has annually stood with a handful of its lapdogs against Cuba against most of the world.

The International Decade for People of African Descent was proclaimed by the UN General Assembly in 2013 by a resolution Proclamation of the International Decade for People of African Descent to be observed around the world from 2015 to 2024.

The conference was co-sponsored by the Cuban Colour Programme against Racism and Racial Discrimination and the Cuba Office of the United Nations Population Fund (UNFPA).

During the decade, groups held activities such as 'Ending Slavery's Legacy of Racism: A Global Imperative for Justice in 2021' and 'Towards Eliminating Systemic Racism and Discrimination

Against People of African Descent in 2023.' The theme for the International Decade was 'People of African descent: Recognition, Justice and Development'.

In November 2019 the Council of Ministers in Cuba approved a national programme against racism and racial discrimination, which aims to combat and definitively eliminate this scourge in Cuban society.

The fact that Cuba introduced a programme to tackle racism was a clear recognition that there was a problem of institutional and individual racism on the island.

In introducing the programme the Cubans recognised that more needed to be done to raise awareness of the prejudices and distorted perceptions of the reality of Afro-Cubans.

Amongst other things, the Cuban authorities recognised that action needed to be taken to deal with racial prejudice in the country's labour market and that much of this came about as a result of accumulated disadvantages associated with ethnic origin and skin colour.

These disadvantages translate into economic and social inequalities and vulnerabilities in Cuban society.

The Cubans committed to doing more to promote anti-racism across society.

Britain

I was born and raised in the Black Country town of Walsall. I was born English and I was born British. But the truth of it is I have never felt either English or British.

I guess I have been reminded far too often during my more than three score years that I don't belong here — despite the place of my birth.

There have been far too many incidents of racism for me just to flick a switch and suddenly feel that I belong. I was aware of the double consciousness before I even knew what it was.

I was introduced to the importance to others of the colour of my skin long before I understood it. My very presence was an affront to some people as I grew up. Not because of anything I had necessarily said or done but simply because I was an African.

There have been too many occasions where my Blackness has been an inconvenience when it comes to decisions over my suitability to be offered a job.

I remember after leaving school and making a call for a building trades job and being invited for an interview. On arrival, it was clear that the office secretary found it highly amusing that someone with a McKenzie surname wasn't white and dressed in a kilt.

This was only surpassed by her boss who spent the entire 'interview' asking me about my relationship with the police and whether I had been involved in any of the uprisings that were taking place at the time.

Needless to say, I did not get the job which might have had something to do with the fact that I took an instant dislike to the place and the racists running it and decided that they needed to hear the truth about what it was like to get stopped and searched virtually every time you left the house.

They also needed to hear my stories of why we as Black people felt the need to take action against police brutality in the way that we did.

I did not have time to tell these racists before I left the office about what it felt like to be chased down the road by racists who wanted to do you serious harm — as I was on more than one occasion. I also didn't tell these people what it felt like to be told that your reaction to constant racism was because we had a collective 'chip on our shoulders'.

It is hard to put into words what it feels like to be subjected to this and know full well that there is literally nobody in a position of authority that you can tell that would give a toss.

The only people you knew would understand would be other Black people because the chances are they would have experienced something similar.

But as I got older I realised that there were people standing up against this racism and that it wasn't just me feeling and experiencing this thing that caused a regular knot deep in my stomach on most days.

I also developed more clarity that Africans did not just land in Britain but that we had been here for some considerable time. This was no mean feat because it was something that was never taught at school.

I found out on my own devices that Africans had been in Britain since the Roman Times — guarding Hadrian's Wall that divided England from Scotland.

I didn't know this — like many descendants of enslaved Africans I spent the formative years of my life believing that we arrived after the Empire Windrush docked at Tilbury Dock in 1948.

In fact for many years British law allowed enslavement overseas, on the torture chamber ships from West Africa and the West Indian plantations.

Inside the British Isles, however, slavery was not legally allowed.

Nobody told me about the case of James Somerset in 1772. Somerset had escaped from his master who then recaptured him in Britain and tried to force him to return to Jamaica.

The Lord Chief Justice ruled that he could not be taken from Britain by force. While in Britain, he was free.

Nobody taught me about the so-called 'Black Loyalists' who had been promised freedom from enslavement if they fought for Britain in the American War of Independence. They were brought to Britain when the British lost the war.

They were left to fend for themselves and many ended up destitute and begging on London's streets.

Some 400 were eventually transported to Sierra Leone in West Africa in a resettlement project by the Committee for the Relief of the Black Poor.

As I began to get involved in the labour and trade union movement I was led to believe that we were new and had no experience of trade unionism or rebellion against exploitation.

I was left to find William Cuffay (from St Kitts in the Caribbean) for myself.

Cuffay was one of the leaders of the Chartist movement who was convicted of preparing to set fire to certain buildings as a signal for an uprising and was transported to Tasmania in 1848.

Many of the Chartists' demands are now an accepted part of our Parliamentary system, such as secret ballots in elections, votes for all and payment to MPs so that not only the rich could stand for election.

There is a need to decolonise education in Britain and to tell the full story of African involvement in Britain and the role we have played in building working-class and peasant resistance to exploitation across the country for centuries.

The arch-racist imperialist Cecil Rhodes, whose atrocities against Africans were never talked about at school, once said: 'To be born English is to win first prize in the lottery of life.'

Closer to home, in 1937, another arch-racist, Winston Churchill, displayed his own master race inclinations when he said: 'I do not believe that the dog in the manger has the right to the manger, simply because he has lain there for so long.

I do not believe that the Red Indian has been wronged in America, or the Black man has been wronged in Australia, simply because they have been displaced by a higher, stronger race.'

To them everything other than white is inferior and to be treated that way. Sadly these were not isolated views and were and are prevalent throughout England.

These statements get to the heart of the conversation I continue to have with myself regarding how much others regard me as English and, therefore having any worth, but, much more importantly, the extent to which I attach Englishness and worth to myself.

By birth I am absolutely English even though I was once told within six inches of my face by some bad-breathed racist that it takes more than birth to make me English.

I am proud to have been born a Black Country boy. Not a piece of land set aside for Black people but an area of the Midlands, with an often contested boundary, that was the centre of the Industrial Revolution.

Those of us coming from the Black Country are very proud of this part of our heritage but many of us have other ancestry from outside the area that we are equally proud to draw on.

The recent weeks of surging racism and prior to that the European football competition have once again sparked in me the vexed question of my Englishness or lack thereof.

I failed the so-called Tebbit test years ago. This was where the former right-wing Tory Secretary of State Norman Tebbit talked about the importance of youth from the former colonies supporting England rather than India, Pakistan or the West Indies etc in cricket matches.

The truth is that I have never supported any English team in any sport at any time.

I guess some of this stems back to the South African-born England cricket captain Tony Greig claiming in 1976 that it was his intention to make the West Indian cricket team 'grovel' during that summer's series in England.

I cannot believe that he did not understand the connotations that would be drawn from the comments of a white South African at the height of apartheid by both the Black community and, of course, white racists.

I remember being at the Saturday session of the Oval Test Match in London watching 'Whispering Death' Michael Holding destroy the English batting, including Greig.

Truthfully it has always been so much more than just about cricket or any other sport.

Perhaps it was the years of being forcefully told that the lovely colour of my skin meant that I couldn't possibly be English, despite the fact of my birth.

Forgive me for never getting over — as some have suggested I should — the stealing of my ancestors from their lives in Africa by the English and their transport in the most horrendous conditions to be in enslavement for hundreds of years — all to enrich English capital.

Or for my own lack of forgiveness for my ancestors being kept in a state of semi-enslavement through the colonial years in Jamaica.

It could be the scars of being spat at and harassed on a daily basis as a five-year-old walking to and from school every day just months after racist Enoch Powell's so-called 'river of blood' speech which he delivered in Birmingham less than ten miles from my home.

I have never really gotten over having my skin rubbed — as man and boy — to see if my colour came off like shoe polish and my hair rubbed and marvelled at how it allegedly resembled cotton wool.

My dilemma certainly has not been helped by being taught to hate myself because I was not white and the effort it took to hide this and the very many years it took me to even like myself despite the flags of St George or the Union Jack being waved in my face as I was threatened with violence.

So please don't talk to me about how I should 'fly the flag'.

When it became apparent that I was failing to join in with whatever the latest display of English nationalism or alleged patriotism was, I would sometimes get called out by friends or work colleagues.

The simple answer is that if you have spent your entire life being told that you are not really English and that you are inferior because of the colour of your skin, it's impossible to just turn a switch and become English for the duration of the match or tournament — even if I wanted to.

I realise that not every Black person feels the same way that I do. That's fine — we are not a monolith — even though I have been often called on to speak on behalf of the thoughts of every person of African descent ever born or likely to be born.

My late parents always told me that I had to be twice as good as everyone else just to be considered the same. I gave up on this quest sometime during my early twenties.

It was already clear to me that it was completely unachievable. Not just because of my own limited capabilities but because far too many people were unable to look beyond the colour of my skin in their judgement of me.

Much later, even during some of the high points in a job sense of my trade union career, I learned of comments made more than once about me only having achieved these positions because of some apparent box-ticking exercise.

In many ways it was a liberation not to be burdened with being bothered about proving myself to anyone but myself. But I would be lying if I didn't say hearing those comments was anything less than hurtful — especially coming from within the labour movement.

Thankfully I no longer lose sleep worrying about it as I work in one of the best jobs I have ever had with some of the very best comrades.

All of this said, whenever I leave England I always look forward to returning home. Maybe it's petty nationalism that I am allergic to and the way that I am expected to demonstrate the same as and when called on to do so?

But I never confuse missing home with a delusion that a country that can do what it did to my ancestors, without the remotest sign of reparations, and will do nothing concrete to bring an end to the long made surge in racism, is a great nation. Because great it is not! But it could be!

So whatever patterned cloth you choose to drape yourself in — whatever your colour — is your business. I will take a pass, thank you very much.

I am a product of my ancestors and everything they went through to allow me to sit here and scratch out these words.

I will never forget or forgive the humiliation often meted out to them and the racism I have seen and endured on the warped basis of a fictional white superiority.

It means I cannot join you in displaying a nationalism or so-called patriotism that my experience tells me will all too quickly be turned against me.

But growing up, nobody could mistake the loud noise being made across the world by the Civil Rights and Black Power Movement as a spark that ignited my wish to learn about the history of Africans across the diaspora.

There were few who were more important to developing a sense of self than Malcolm X.

Malcolm X

February 21 should always be heralded as an important day for those of African descent across the globe. It is the anniversary of the murder of Malcolm X.

The fact that his three daughters were forced to launch a $100 million (around £80 million) legal case against the CIA, FBI and the New York Police Department is a reminder that there is unfinished business relating to the killing.

The case alleges that the agencies mentioned, and others, were involved in the murder plot and did nothing to stop the killing of this unparalleled fighter for Black rights.

From day one of the murder and for the six subsequent decades questions have been raised about who was actually responsible for the murder of Malcolm X as he spoke to several hundred people at New York's Audubon Ballroom.

Three men were convicted of crimes in the death but two were exonerated in 2021 after investigators concluded that much of the evidence that convicted them was unreliable.

Authorities were also accused of holding back vital information.

In fact the legal action may have come sooner but the defendants in the case are also accused of withholding information from Malcolm X's family, including the identities of undercover 'informants, agents and provocateurs' and what they knew about the planning that preceded the attack.

There is no doubt that there needs to be more clarity provided to Malcolm's family and over what actually happened and who was really behind his killing.

The excellent 2020 six-part Netflix documentary 'Who Killed Malcolm X?' should take a lot of credit for shedding new light on the murder.

The documentary follows the 30-year investigation carried out by part-time historian Abdur-Rahman Muhammad, a tour guide in Washington DC.

He investigates the allegations made by Talmadge Hayer, a convicted assassin of Malcolm, that the two men convicted alongside him were innocent. He also alleges that his four co-conspirators — Benjamin Thomas, Leon Davis, William X and one other person — were all part of the Nation of Islam mosque in Newark.

After the documentary was released the Manhattan district attorney agreed to carry out a preliminary investigation into the murder of Malcolm.

The DA also announced that the convictions of Muhammad A Aziz and Khalil Islam, who had both served 20 years for the murder would be thrown out because of the new information gathered by Muhammad's investigation.

In 2022 the men were awarded a combined total of $36 million (nearly £29 million) for wrongful imprisonment.

There are clearly many truths that need to be told about the killing of Malcolm but I want to concentrate here on celebrating this inspirational man and in particular his visit to Britain shortly before he was prematurely forced to join the ancestors.

I remember the first time I read *The Autobiography of Malcolm X* (1965). I did so in just a few sittings. I put the book down and the very next day started reading it all over again.

I recall that after each reading of the book I felt 10 feet tall and that no racist should dare to take the foolish step of bothering me in any way.

This was no small empty thought in Walsall back in the day and certainly not in the early 1980s when I first read the autobiography.

The stopping and searching of young Black people by the police was an everyday experience for many of us. So was being attacked by either the National Front or the Ku Klux Klan which had surfaced in the Black Country at the time — listen to the excellent song by Steel Pulse on the iconic Handsworth Revolution album.

It wasn't until some time after reading the book that I found out that Malcolm had passed just a few short miles from my home when he visited Smethwick in the West Midlands, on February 12, days before his murder — coincidentally the same date as I am sitting to begin writing this book.

Malcolm had been invited to Smethwick by Avtar Singh Jouhl, the general secretary of the Indian Workers Association, who was later to become a close friend and comrade.

Conservative MP Peter Griffiths had won the Smethwick seat the year before with the slogan 'If you want a n..... for a neighbour, vote Labour'.

The Labour incumbent, shadow home secretary Patrick Gordon Walker, lost his seat in one of the most racist election campaigns in British history.

When the defeated Walker left Smethwick Town Hall after the vote count the Conservative supporters screamed at him: 'Where are your n...... now, Walker?' and 'Take your n...... away!'

Racism was a defining fact of life around the Black Country at the time and Smethwick was no different. It defined where you could go and what you could do.

Many bars and pubs had signs displayed in windows warning that 'No Coloureds' were allowed.

Marshall Street in Smethwick was especially racist with residents lobbying the council to buy up empty houses along the street and make them available only to white people.

The then Tory Council agreed to the demands of the racists to stop Black people from moving in. Black families were prevented from purchasing or renting properties on Marshall Street and the situation carried on for several years.

Malcolm visited Marshall Street and a local school in February 1965 and told the few press who turned up to see the world-renowned Black leader that he was 'disturbed by reports that coloured people in Smethwick are being treated badly.'

He added: 'I was in Birmingham, Alabama, the other day. This will give me a chance to see if Birmingham, England, is any different.'

Many years later Jouhl told me that Malcolm was appalled by the segregation he witnessed in Smethwick.

Malcolm was an inspiration to those of us like me who were trying to find their feet and voice in the labour and trade union movement.

Towards the end of his life Malcolm was very clear about the importance of Black and white unity not just to defeat racism but to create a new society.

But, specifically, he taught us as Black people that we had worth and that we should always carry ourselves with pride.

I remember someone describing Malcolm as a 'master teacher' and that there was no greater loss to a community than the loss of a master teacher. He was such a loss to people of African descent across the globe.

At Malcolm's funeral, actor and activist Ossie Davis said: 'Malcolm was our manhood, our living, Black manhood. This was his meaning to his people. In honouring him we honour the best in ourselves.'

Though he is no longer with us in physical form, his teaching, example and his spirit still guide us. Our collective spirit demands full disclosure over who was involved in slaying this giant in his prime.

Rivers of Blood and Black Resistance

The face and voice given to racism during the period of the 1960s and early 70s continued to be Enoch Powell, the Birmingham-born former Conservative Party Health Minister.

This further served to push Black workers towards self-organisation. Powell had, as a Health Minister, been responsible for organising immigration from the former British colonies to provide cheap labour for the National Health Service.

Powell is perhaps best known for the infamous speech at Birmingham in April 1968. During the speech he used wild imagery to predict that rivers of blood would flow in Britain if immigration from the former colonies were allowed to continue.

The speech and its aftermath — which included London dockworkers and Smithfield meat porters (who were strongly organised in trade unions) marching in support of Powell — did not go unanswered by Black workers.

The Black Peoples' Alliance (BPA) was formed in 1968 at a meeting in central England at Leamington Spa in Warwickshire. It was a direct response by Black workers to the Powell speech. This alliance of over fifty Black organisations brought together activists of African, African Caribbean and Asian descent.

There was no argument between these groups over the validity of the term 'black'. Black, as the activist and editor of *Race and Class* A. Sivanandan said, 'is not the colour of our skin but the colour of our politics'.

Powell, and others, did not rely solely on questions of culture or notions of racial supremacy as an excuse for stirring up racism. As Lunn argues:

'…expressions of racial hostility were closely tied to questions of employment and of political perspective. Mixed with the vague xenophobia of the time were specific dimensions of institutional racism and of scapegoating, but within a particular set of social, economic and political circumstances'.

In 1969 the BPA organised a march of more than 7000 people to demand that the various pieces of legislation that were being proposed to effectively halt immigration from Black Commonwealth countries should be dropped.

This was the largest Black-led demonstration in Britain to that date.

There were warnings by Black groups taking part in the march of the dire consequences of the failure by the authorities to deal with racism of which the increasingly restrictive immigration legislation of the time was but an expression.

Uprising as Resistance

The rise of unemployment in the major Western industrialized economies during the latter part of the 1970s and early 80s, and the election of two true believers in Margaret Thatcher, in Britain and Ronald Reagan, in the US, was the signal for right-wing economist Milton Friedman that he could carry out his experiment on two of the largest stages of all.

The social policies of the monetarists had a particularly devastating impact on all working-class people in the UK with unemployment levels, for example, reaching around 4 million by some counts.

However it was the Black community that was especially hard hit. This was more pronounced for the Black community when taken alongside a number of other key indicators of racism.

The Thatcher government placed a great emphasis on law and order and gave the police the laws by which they could apply their power. However, this emphasis on law and order did not seem to extend as far as the perpetrators of racist attacks against the Black community.

What did happen was that the racism within the police force, particularly in the inner cities, was exposed by their use of controversial strategies such as 'stop and search' or 'being a suspected person (sus)'.

The Black community could not even find a space for relaxation at events such as professional football matches.

The football grounds of England were becoming no-go zones for many in the Black community because of the level of racism directed towards the few Black players who were plying their trade in the professional game.

The same harassment of Black players spilled onto the terraces with the police making no attempts during the 1970s and for most of the 1980s to tackle the problem.

The terraces were breeding grounds for fascist organisations such as the National Front who then took their hatred into local communities.

The toxic brew of high levels of unemployment and harassment, including from the police, was a recipe for disaster. It was also, as history has shown, and I have documented throughout this book, inevitable that Black people would eventually resist the racism that they were experiencing.

The resistance revealed itself as street uprisings in the inner city areas of St. Paul's in Bristol, during April 1980, followed by Brixton in South London (April 1981) and, later Toxteth in Liverpool as well as Southall in West London.

Lord Scarman was appointed by the Thatcher Government to lead an inquiry into the riots in Brixton. Brixton was particularly significant as it was widely held to be the spiritual home of the Black community.

It was also the place where there had been the most damage to property caused (around £10 million). The Inquiry was charged with examining both the immediate and underlying causes of, what the Government called 'disturbances' and many in the Black community termed an 'uprising'.

Scarman, after taking evidence from key players such as the police, the police and community groups held that poor housing and lack of employment opportunities were contributory factors.

However, Scarman also condemned the racist behaviour of some police officers while falling short of labelling the whole of the Metropolitan Police as racists.

Scarman's recommendations included the appointment of more Black police officers, improved police training, an independent element in the police complaints procedure and a rationalisation of the SUS laws.

For many in the Black community these recommendations failed to tackle the fundamental problem. That problem was not only a lack of police accountability or the lack of Black officers, it was fundamentally a lack of power for Black people to be able to influence their lives either in their communities or, if they were lucky enough to have a job, in the workplace.

Jamaica

My parents were both born and reared on the Caribbean island of Jamaica.

They were very proud of being from Jamaica. They, like many Jamaicans of their age group, balked at being identified as Jamaican.

I remember watching the West Indies play cricket against England as a youngster and my mom telling me off for supporting the West Indies. She said I was born in England and should be supporting the likes of Geoffrey Boycott over the *Master Blaster* Viv Richards. Really?

It was one of the rare occasions when my Dad had the better political instincts and knew exactly why I was supporting the West Indies.

It was a question of Black pride — something my mom usually better understood. Dad was clear that cricket was more than a sport. It was a chance to beat the former colonial ruler.

Aside from that who really wouldn't prefer watching Richards, Gordon Greenidge, Desmond Haynes, Malcolm Marshall, Holding and 'Big Bird' Joel Garner over England — even with the great Ian Botham.

So even though I wasn't born there I always saw Jamaica as the 'home' that racists always encouraged me to go back to.

The first inhabitants of Jamaica were the Arawaks (also called the Taino).

They had migrated from South America some four centuries before Columbus 'discovered' Jamaica on 4 May 1494.

They named the island Xaymaca, which means 'land of wood and water'.

Then Christopher Columbus turned up in 1494 and arrogantly claimed the island for Spain.

In 1503, Columbus spent a year shipwrecked there. The Spanish crown granted the island to the Columbus family.

Under Columbus, the Spanish did not make much use of the island until 1509 when Juan de Esquivel founded the first permanent European settlement, the town of Sevilla la Nueva (New Seville), what is now St Ann's Bay on the north coast.

In 1534, the capital was moved to Villa de la Vega (later Santiago de la Vega), now called Spanish Town.

Spanish colonial rule lasted for over 150 years, during which time they enslaved the Taino population and eventually wiped them out through forced labour and diseases to which they had no resistance.

The Spanish then began importing Africans to work on the island's plantations.

Unable to find gold and other precious metals in Jamaica, the Spanish saw little use for the island. This period of relative neglect created a power vacuum that would soon be exploited by other European powers, most notably the British.

In 1655, British naval forces led by Admiral William Penn and General Robert Venables captured Jamaica from the Spanish. The Spanish were forced to surrender, freeing their slaves and fleeing to Cuba.

These freed slaves became known as the Maroons who would play a significant role in the island's future.

Jamaica was taken over by the English in 1670 under the provisions of the Treaty of Madrid.

During the final decades of the 17th century, growing numbers of English immigrants arrived; the sugar, cacao, and other agricultural and forest industries were rapidly expanded, and the consequent demand for plantation labour led to the large-scale importation of enslaved Africans.

Enslaved Africans were forced to work the plantations of wealthy Englishmen, many of whom lived in England, lavishly spending their Jamaican profits.

The British capitalised on Jamaica's strategic location in the Caribbean to challenge Spanish dominance and disrupt their trade routes.

Port Royal, once an insignificant town, quickly became a haven for British privateers and pirates, including the infamous Sir Henry Morgan. The wealth amassed through piracy transformed Port Royal into the 'wickedest city in the world' during the 17th century.

However, Port Royal's fortunes changed dramatically in 1692 when a massive earthquake destroyed much of the city. The survivors relocated to Kingston, which became Jamaica's capital in 1872.

The quake tilted two-thirds of the city into the sea, and a tidal wave swept away the debris and a great deal of valuable loot. Divers have turned up some of the bounties, but much remains in the reefs off Kingston's shore.

Throughout all of these events, resistance was fertile.

The Maroons established their own communities in Jamaica's mountainous interior. They fiercely resisted British attempts to subdue them, embracing guerrilla warfare tactics and exploiting their knowledge of the island's terrain.

In 1739 and 1740, after two major Maroon Wars, the British signed treaties with the Maroons, granting them land and rights as free men.

In return, the Maroons agreed to cease hostilities and assist in recapturing runaway slaves. This agreement, however, caused divisions within the Maroon communities, as not all members agreed to return escaped slaves to the plantations.

As the British expanded their control over Jamaica, the island's economy became increasingly reliant on the plantation system, with sugar production at its heart.

The demand for labour led to an escalation in the trade in human beings with thousands of enslaved Africans being forced over to Jamaica to endure brutal conditions on the plantations.

Throughout this period, enslaved Africans resisted oppression through acts of defiance and rebellion. Some slaves managed to escape and join the Maroons, while others staged uprisings, such as the 1760 Easter Rebellion led by Tacky and the 1831 Christmas Rebellion led by Sam Sharpe.

These acts of resistance, combined with growing opposition to slavery from humanitarian groups in Britain, eventually led to the Slave Trade Act calling for the abolition of the slave trade in 1807 and the emancipation of slaves in 1838.

The British Parliament abolished slavery on 1 August 1834. The act made available around £24 million as compensation to the owners of the nearly 310,000 liberated Africans on the island.

But without slave labour the sugarcane plantations were no longer so profitable, and it seemed their time had also passed.

Competition and falling prices took a further toll on Jamaica's sugar production reign.

Large numbers of the freed Africans abandoned the plantations following emancipation and took possession of unoccupied lands in the interior, gravely disrupting the economy.

Labour shortages, bankrupt plantations, and declining trade resulted in a protracted economic crisis. Oppressive taxation, discriminatory acts by the courts, and land-exclusion measures ultimately caused widespread unrest among Blacks.

Whilst the slave owners were compensated for their lost 'property', and continued to live in opulence, freed Africans suffered economic hardship. A drought in 1865 added to the hardship.

In 1865, the Morant Bay Rebellion erupted.

Led by Paul Bogle, protesters stormed the Morant Bay Courthouse and killed several white officials.

The British authorities responded with brutal force, executing hundreds of people and destroying thousands of homes.

This event marked a turning point in Jamaica's history, leading to the introduction of the Crown Colony system of government, which centralised power in the hands of the British governor.

Jamaica's becoming a crown colony meant losing the large degree of self-government it had been given since the late 17th century.

Due to the strife, the Jamaican Assembly relinquished much of its power to the governor, and in 1866, Jamaica became an official Crown Colony. Representative government was partly restored in 1884.

Jamaica gained a degree of local political control in the late 1930s and held its first election under full universal adult suffrage in 1944.

In the early 20th century, there was an increasing push for self-government in Jamaica, fuelled by dissatisfaction with the Crown Colony system and the hardships faced by the island's population.

In 1938, widespread unrest and strikes led to the formation of the first labour unions and political parties.

The Bustamante Industrial Trade Union (BITU), founded by Alexander Bustamante and the National Workers' Union, founded by Norman Manley played pivotal roles in Jamaica's journey towards self-rule.

The first general elections under Universal Adult Suffrage were held in 1944, marking a significant step towards independence.

Jamaica joined nine other British territories in the West Indies Federation in 1958.

The federation aimed to promote regional unity. However, this arrangement was short-lived, as Jamaicans voted against continued membership in a 1961 referendum. This move led to the eventual collapse of the federation.

Bustamante, who became prime minister when Jamaica achieved full independence, urged Jamaica's withdrawal from the federation.

On August 6, 1962, Jamaica finally achieved independence from Britain with a new constitution enshrining its citizens' rights and freedoms. This event marked the culmination of centuries of resistance by the Jamaican people but, as with so many others at the time, was largely a 'flag independence.'

Jamaica was still largely under British control with the Monarch being the head of state.

I have visited the island on a number of occasions but nothing will ever replace the first time that I visited as a young child with my mother, brother and sister in 1974.

Jamaica is a beautiful place but it faces many problems including deep levels of poverty.

After reaching a historic low of 9.9 per cent in 2007, poverty more than doubled to 24.6 per cent in 2013 following the Global Financial Crisis.

The rate fell again to 11 per cent in 2019 as the economy recovered, only to spike back to an estimated 21 per cent in 2020 due to the Covid-19 pandemic.

By 2021 the poverty rate reached 16.7 per cent. These dramatic ups and downs highlight the country's vulnerability to economic shocks in a nation so deeply dependent on the tourism industry and agriculture.

Tourism in particular is highly sensitive to global disruptions, whilst agriculture faces frequent climate-related challenges.

This reliance has limited economic diversification and sustained growth, with Jamaica's real GDP growing at an annual average of only 0.8 per cent from 1990 to 2019—below the Latin America and Caribbean regional average of 2.7 per cent.

Although job creation programmes have helped reduce poverty in some periods, many of these jobs are insecure and concentrated in low-productivity sectors like tourism and retail.

The lack of job security leaves workers highly susceptible to economic downturns. During the Covid-19 pandemic, unemployment surged from 7.3 per cent to 12.6 per cent in just six months, exposing the fragility of many households' livelihoods.

The country also faces major obstacles in healthcare and education. Access to both is highly dependent on the place you occupy in society. For example malnutrition is three times more common in low-income households.

Although perhaps not receiving the attention garnered by Marxists on the US continent there have been scholars and activists in Jamaica who have sought to bring attention to these inequalities. They have sought to put forward a socialist alternative to the dominant neo-liberal philosophy followed by far too many Caribbean governments.

Prominent amongst these pioneers is the great Jamaican Marxist historian and activist Richard Hart.

Richard Hart

Some people reading this will be unfamiliar with Hart's work but that's about to be put right and hopefully this towering but gentle man can be more widely remembered and learnt from.

Hart was born in Jamaica in 1917 and was one of the foremost pioneers of Marxism in Jamaica.

I met Hart in London during the late part of the last century when my comrade and sister Mary Davis introduced me to this charming man.

Within a few short minutes of speaking to him I quickly realised and was embarrassed that I knew nothing of the political struggles in Jamaica, the country that was the birthplace of my parents.

It came as a shock to me that I clearly knew far more about the US

Civil Rights movement and Malcolm X than I did about somewhere where my family had blood in the game.

So I started doing my research and after devouring everything that Hart had written I decided that he deserved to be read alongside the works on Caribbean history and politics by CLR James and Eric Williams.

Higher praise than that I am unable to give.

His book, *The Slaves Who Abolished Slavery: Black in Rebellion*, is a really important book that should be read by all activists — Black or white.

As accessible as anything you will ever read on the enslavement of Africans, the book leads the reader to an understanding that it was the enslaved themselves who did more than anyone to make the brutal inhumane system unworkable.

It was not the work of abolitionists such as William Wilberforce that was the decisive factor in the ending of enslavement. That honour belonged to the enslaved themselves — some of whom, I am proud to say, would have been my ancestors.

It was no small thing for someone to relate the idea that the rebellions of enslaved Africans — such as the ones mentioned earlier in this chapter — were not isolated incidents but were in fact endemic.

But writing down, as Hart did, that Black people had agency in our own liberation was a revolutionary act in itself.

It would have been hard reading for many, including some on the left, who believed with their saviour complex that enslavement and colonialism were ended mainly because of the no doubt brave intervention of white campaigners.

Hart was one of the founding members of Jamaica's social democratic People's National Party in 1938 alongside Norman Manley who served as its president until his death in 1969.

Hart served as a member of the PNP national executive committee from 1941 until 1952. A year before being elected to the EC, Hart was arrested by the British colonial powers for having the audacity to help organise a protest demanding the release of trade union leader Alexander Bustamante.

Bustamante's crime was attempting to form a trade union, a task in which Hart was assisting.

The trade union leader, who founded the Jamaica Labour Party in 1943, would later become the country's first chief minister — the head of pre-independence Jamaica's government — in 1953.

Hart was a committed trade unionist as a means of organising and raising the living standards of Jamaicans still suffering in the harsh aftermath of enslavement and the brutal British colonial regime.

He served as Assistant Secretary of the Caribbean Labour Congress from 1945 to 1953.

Hart, an unapologetic Marxist, was imprisoned without trial by what was long regarded as a ruthless British colonial administration in Jamaica.

In 1954 Hart, along with Frank Hill, Ken Hill and Arthur Henry — known as 'the four Hs', was expelled from the PNP for their Marxist views.

But Hart continued to play a leading role in the politics of the island leading up to independence in 1962.

Like many on the left in Jamaica, such as leading academic and activist Trevor Munroe, Hart was concerned that the country was in a state of 'constitutional decolonisation', rather than fully freeing itself from British colonial rule.

The British monarchy is still the head of the Jamaican state with the final court of appeal in the country being the Judicial Committee of the British Privy Council.

Moves to shift the final vestiges of British colonial rule by removing the Monarch as Jamaica's head of state are gathering pace with cross-party agreement between the ruling Jamaica Labour Party and the opposition PNP. A referendum on the subject is expected soon and is expected to easily pass.

Hart's excellent work: *Towards Decolonisation: Political, Labour and Economic Developments in Jamaica 1938–1945* describes the process of decolonisation from a Marxist viewpoint.

This is well worth a read for all those who throw around terms such as decolonising. What is required is a fundamental change in society, not a few ragtag artificial changes.

After a stint in Guyana for two years from 1963, where he edited the Mirror newspaper, which supported the legendary Cheddi Jagan,

Hart moved to London in 1965 and co-founded the Caribbean Labour Solidarity in 1974 with key activists such as Cleston Taylor and Lionel Jeffrey.

Hart remained the Honorary President of CLS until his passing in 2013.

He went on to serve as attorney-general in the revolutionary government of Grenada after the New Jewel Movement was successful in overthrowing the US-backed regime of Eric Gairy in 1979.

Hart spent his final years in Britain where he became a close ally of the Communist Party of Britain.

He died in Bristol on December 21, 2013 as a true inspiration to many of us of Caribbean heritage.

He is someone whose contribution to Marxist thought and action in the Caribbean and Britain needs to be more widely appreciated. What I remembered most from that visit was the deep levels of poverty in Jamaica and the undeniable fact that no matter how much most people I met were full of love, people were struggling to survive.

This was a lesson brought to this country as many made the trip to help rebuild Britain after World War II but, of course, meaning that the people needed to build the economy of Jamaica in the aftermath of enslavement and the ending years of colonialism had left for the cold and grey shores of another island.

Since its independence in 1962, Jamaica, an island of around 2.8 million people, has spent most of its time under the strictures of one International Monetary Fund programme or another.

On independence from the British colonial ruler, the country inherited a dependence on exporting cash crops such as sugar, coffee and cocoa.

This was an unsustainable situation for the economy as was the later over-dependence on tourism as the main source of wealth for the country.

Jamaica was forced to run to the IMF for 'support'.

IMF programmes are, of course, far from being some benign helping hand to struggling economies. They are ruthless means of imposing neoliberal policies at the expense of the working and peasant classes.

One IMF programme in 2010 saw Jamaica borrowing $850 million from 2010 to 2012.

One of the IMF's conditions was wage freezes for public sector workers in 2010 and 2011, which given inflation, amounted to a 20 per cent real terms cut.

Jamaica now owes agencies such as the IMF and World Bank as well as foreign governments something in the region of $60 billion (£48 billion).

Jamaica will never be able to pay this money back and will be on a permanent treadmill of making money to repay debt as the poor get poorer.

If there is a genuine interest in tackling the serious issues faced by Jamaica, such as the deeply ingrained poverty, health emergencies such as the Covid-19 pandemic or climate change then the debt should simply be cancelled.

Last year Jamaican authorities announced that poverty levels were around 17 per cent — a rise of 5.7 per cent of the survey reported two years earlier.

Rural areas suffered the highest rates of poverty at around 22.1 per cent with urban areas hitting 15.5 per cent. Poverty rates in the capital Kingston are around 10.5 per cent.

Poverty levels have been made worse by the Covid-19 pandemic which, in common with many places across the globe, severely impacted the ability of people to go out and make a living.

Around 60 per cent of Jamaica's employment is informal. Living hand to mouth and knowing that if you don't work then you don't eat is a way of life for most of the population.

The Jamaica of the Marley movie was on the verge of civil war. Now people of this beautiful island learn to live with the violence and decide which areas they can safely travel through.

I am not sure that my grandmother would have been able to run a small shop now in Trench Town as she did back in the day. It is also not certain that I would even be able to safely visit her.

The Jamaica of the 2020s has a murder rate of more than 40 per 100,000 — making it one of the most violent places on the planet — with gang violence accounting for 70 per cent of killings.

But Jamaica has volunteered to send an armed police force to its near neighbour Haiti, presumably to pass on its (lack of) expertise in how to fight the gang violence that has left much of that Caribbean nation in the grip of violent gangs.

Just two years ago Prime Minister Andrew Holness, of the JLP, was forced to declare a state of emergency for parts of Kingston and some central and western parishes, including Montego Bay, because of soaring gang violence. The move gave the notoriously gun-happy police powers to carry out arrests without warrants.

Things do not appear to have radically changed since the era depicted in the Marley movie.

Much like during the 1970s gangs are still fighting over the scant resources available to them as the super-rich funnel the wealth created by the tourism industry out of the country.

I have nothing against free musical gigs that aim to bring people together or even just to feel better.

But this will not be enough to improve the lives of the Jamaican working and peasant classes who have simply not shared in the prosperity that the island's ruling class and their international capitalist partners have achieved.

Hoping to become the next superstar Bob Marley is a great ambition to have. But it will take solidarity to support the growth of the trade union and socialist movement on the island that will really make a difference.

As they sit in their luxurious homes on the hill looking down on the people struggling to survive, the ruling political elite of Jamaica has offered no real strategy for tackling poverty on the island and the gang violence that has spawned it.

Mexico

Most people do not imagine that Mexico has a sizable population of Africans. I certainly didn't before beginning the research for this book.

Mexico has its own complex racial history, shaped by colonialism, racial mixing and colourism. Racism exists, but functions with its distinct social and cultural characteristics.

African-Mexicans along with the indigenous communities face far higher rates of poverty than anyone else.

African-Mexicans face huge challenges. Despite growing recognition of Mexico's African heritage, racism persists.

More than a million people in Mexico are descended from enslaved Africans and identify as 'Black', 'dark' or 'African-Mexican'.

But beyond the southern state of Oaxaca they are little-known and the community's leaders are now warning of possible radical steps to achieve official recognition.

Afro-Mexicans have been living in the Costa Chica area, on the Pacific coast of Oaxaca, since their ancestors were forced from Africa during the 16th century as enslaved human beings.

New Spain, as Mexico was then called, brought an estimated 200,000 enslaved Africans to the region.

The port of Veracruz, which borders the Caribbean, was the primary arrival point for these ships and as a result, the city continues to reflect a strong African influence in its music, dance, cultures, and food.

In 1570, Gaspar Yanga led a revolt and after a successful escape settled in the highlands.

By 1600, his settlement had joined with another group of escaped slaves led by Francisco de la Matosa, and for decades they resisted capture from Spanish colonialists.

In 1618, Yanga negotiated with Spanish officials to grant freedom to the fugitive slaves and independence to their village, which became known as San Lorenzo de los Negros.

In 1932, the small town changed its name to honour its founder and is now known as Yanga in the state of Veracruz. In 2017, Yanga became a UNESCO World Heritage site.

A statue of Gaspar Yanga along with a plaque now stands in the town square. Every year on 10 August, Yanga holds a carnival to celebrate Gaspar Yanga's legacy.

Mexico became the first country in North America to have a Black president in 1829, more than 175 years before the election of Barack Obama.

Born to an African-Mexican father and Indigenous-Mexican mother, Vicente Guerrero fought in the Mexican Revolution for 11 years, eventually helping the country gain independence from Spanish rule.

He became president in 1829 and instituted sweeping policy changes, including benefits to the working class and Indigenous and taxes on the rich.

It was under Guerrero that slavery in Mexico was abolished on September 16, 1829 (which is now recognised as Mexico's Independence Day), approximately 40 years before the US would do the same.

Of course the move angered US slaveholders and ultimately resulted in Guerrero's downfall. In 1830, he was forcefully removed from office and returned to the southern Mexican states to organise another rebellion.

During that uprising he was captured by Minister of War José Antonio Facio and taken into custody in Oaxaca for trial. He was executed on February 14, 1831.

Though Guerrero had petitioned for a southern state separate from Mexico, it wasn't until 1849 that the state of Guerrero was created and named after him.

The state's motto is 'My Motherland Comes First', which was said by Guerrero in his refusal to surrender to Spanish rule. Today Vicente Guerrero's remains are held in the Monumento a la Independencia in Mexico City to recognise his role in the country's independence.

Despite this rich history, African-Mexicans only became recognised as an ethnic identity in a preliminary census in 2015. This gave 1.38 million African-Mexicans the opportunity to self-identify for the first time.

The Costa Chica region, which encompasses the southern states of Guerrero and Oaxaca has the largest concentration of African-Mexican citizens.

Historically, African-Mexicans have faced discrimination on multiple fronts in Mexico. To this day, many live in regions with lower economic conditions and limited access to resources.

For instance, the lack of roads in Costa Chica, a region spanning parts of Oaxaca and Guerrero where a significant portion of the African-Mexican population lives, limits economic opportunities.

The main sources of income for locals — fishing and agriculture — are increasingly threatened by climate change, further exacerbating the region's economic challenges.

African-Mexican communities face limited access to education, healthcare and even the internet. In 2020, for example, over 83,000 African descendants between the ages of 3 and 17 across Mexico were not attending school.

Colombia

Colombia has one of the largest populations of Africans in Latin America.

During the conquest and subsequent colonial rule, indigenous populations in Colombia became slaves to both Spanish settlers and Creole elites.

In common with large parts of the Americas, much of the Indigenous population of what is now known as Colombia was wiped out by the Spanish as a result of the disgraceful labour conditions they were forced to work under and the European diseases against which they had no immunity.

In 1512, the Spanish crown attempted to regulate slavery through the Laws of Burgos. Later, in 1542, the New Laws aimed to provide better treatment to indigenous populations, even proposing a ban on their enslavement. However, these legal measures had limited impact.

With the decline in the Indigenous population West Africans were forced to come to the region between the 16th and 18th centuries as enslaved labour on plantations.

Enslaved Africans mounted frequent rebellions against the slave owners.

During 1530 a slave rebellion in Santa Marta destroyed the town. The city would be rebuilt only to suffer a new rebellion in the 1550s.

Although it was possible in Colombia for an individual slave to flee their masters and go unnoticed among the free Black population of a large city, it was a precarious situation in which the fugitive was at constant risk of discovery.

Many therefore joined communities of Maroons where they could find more security.

In some cases the threat of revolt by enslaved Africans was used as a sort of collective bargaining to secure improvements.

In 1768 in the province of Santa Marta a group of enslaved Africans wounded a foreman whom they accused of ill-treatment, when their master sent a couple of white men to subdue them, the Africans killed one of them.

Far from being intimidated, the rebels gave their master an ultimatum, if he did not agree to their demands they would burn down the entire estate and escape to live with the 'brave Indians'.

The master accepted their demands, swearing to forgive them for the revolt, stopping the mistreatment and agreeing that if the slaves were ever sold this should be done collectively so as not to divide the families.

The owner also agreed to provide the workers with a good quantity of tobacco and brandy as compensation for the abuses.

Similar incidents occurred in Neiva in 1773 and Cucuta in 1780.

The Africans had reached an agreement with the Jesuit priests so that their status was more akin to that of free peasants in a sharecropping with some recompense for their crops and even some guaranteed holidays.

When a new master refused to abide by the deal the Africans rebelled and successfully demanded that the colonial government authorities recognise their rights.

But the most famous slave rebellion was that of the slaves of San Basilio de Palenque, led by Benkos Biohó.

The rebellion was so successful that on August 23, 1691, the king of Spain was forced to issue a certificate ordering the general freedom of the Palenques and their right to land.

At the end of the 17th century, the colonial authorities tried again to start a great campaign against the Maroons but despite succeeding in destroying some villages, the campaign failed as the African communities managed to preserve their freedom and moved southwards.

The 1851 abolition triggered significant political upheavals. The excluded population joined liberal social foundations, contributing to land seizures. The period also saw the abolition of the death penalty and freedom of expression.

The abolition of slavery in Colombia preceded Abraham Lincoln's

Emancipation Proclamation in the United States by twelve years, occurring in 1863.

Despite legal abolition, modern challenges persist, with various social sectors highlighting contemporary forms of exploitation.

According to a post-census survey, the government estimates that Africans constitute 10 per cent of the total population, which is moving towards 5 million African descendants.

This figure is disputed by some who say the figure is much more like between 36-40 per cent.

Francia Márquez Mina, the first African woman Vice President of Colombia, argues that there are about 15 million African descendants in Colombia.

Africans are present in every major city in the country. It is thought that there are around one million living in the capital Bogota.

Coastal regions of Colombia can have significant Afro-Colombian populations that are as high as 90 per cent in the case of the Pacific or 60 per cent on the Atlantic coast.

The department of Valle del Cauca has the most Africans followed by Bolivar, Antioquia, Narino and Choco.

The combined total of the first three of these departments with the highest number of Africans amounts to 59.2 per cent of the country's African population.

Colombia has adopted legal provisions, policies and strategies and set up institutions to protect human rights and address violations.

But much more needs to be done to effectively transform their daily lives, by tackling high levels of poverty, ensuring security, education, housing, employment, access to basic services, freedom of movement, access to justice, participation in political and public affairs, adequate representation, self-governance and land rights.

Many Africans have detailed the violence, including sexual and gender-based violence and rape that they have been subjected to. Prior to the current administration of Gustavo Petro little was done to tackle these issues.

After centuries of rights violations, Colombia must ensure structure and institutional reform that will ensure people of African descent in the country can exercise their rights fully and freely.

Canada

If you listened to the wrong people you could easily fall into the trap that Canada was a land of milk and honey where everyone — regardless of their background or colour — was treated with dignity and respect.

This of course is utter nonsense.

The notion of Canada as a tolerant, multicultural society is as real as Fantasy Island.

The fictional tale told about Canada is clearly designed to conceal the realities of this deeply divided nation not only from people looking in but also to create a false world for those living there who would prefer not to look.

Although my focus in this book is Africa and Africans I want to use this space to acknowledge the genocide committed against the indigenous peoples of the land now known as Canada. The final book in this trilogy will return in more detail to their plight.

But when the Europeans arrived in the late 15th and early 16th centuries it is estimated that around two million people already lived there.

Much of that population was wiped out in short order In much the same way as other indigenous communities were on that side of the Atlantic.

In the early 1600s the colony of New France was founded in what is now known as Canada. The enslavement of Africans and Indigenous peoples was common on the territory.

King Louis XIV authorised the enslavement of Africans for the new territory as far back as 1689. New France passed specific laws in 1709 that legalised slavery thereby categorising enslaved people as property with no rights.

A set of regulations known as the Code Noir were put in place in most French colonies and are likely to have been in place in New France.

The Code Noir consisted of sixty articles that regulated the life, death, purchase, religion, and treatment of enslaved people by their masters in all French colonies.

It provided that the slaves should be baptised and educated in the Catholic faith. It prohibited masters from making their slaves work on Sundays and religious holidays.

It required that slaves be clothed, fed and taken care of when sick. It prohibited slaves from owning property and stated that they had no legal capacity.

It also governed their marriages, their burials, their punishments, and the conditions they had to meet in order to gain their freedom.

But article 32 of the code is instructive enough.

It read: 'The runaway slave shall have his ears cut off, and shall be branded with the fleur de lis on the shoulder. On the third offence, he shall suffer death.'

Despite the potential penalties many enslaved people, as we have seen elsewhere, refused to merely submit to their condition.

Many fought back by running away or by helping others to escape.

In 1777, by which time Britain had taken control of the territory, thousands of enslaved Africans fled from British North America into the state of Vermont, which had abolished slavery during that year.

Amongst many acts of defiance to the enslavement of Africans in Canada that of Chloe Cooley must be mentioned.

Enslaved in Upper Canada, Cooley's courageous struggle against her enslavement in 1793 set in motion the earliest legal challenge to slavery in British North America.

Her defiance led to the passing of the Act to Limit Slavery in Upper Canada, marking the first legislative restriction on slavery in the British Empire.

Cooley was enslaved by Sergeant Adam Vrooman, a United Empire Loyalist. As opposition to slavery grew in Canada, many enslavers sought to sell their slaves across the border before new regulations could be enacted.

On March 14, 1793, Cooley resisted her owner's attempt to sell her in New York State.

Vrooman and his accomplices violently restrained Cooley, tying her up and dragging her to a boat on the Niagara River. Witnesses later described how she screamed and fought back, struggling against the men who sought to sell her away from her home.

Peter Martin, a Black Loyalist and free man, along with William Grisley, a White resident, witnessed the horrific event and reported it to Lieutenant-Governor John Graves Simcoe.

Simcoe, the first Lieutenant-Governor of Upper Canada and a known abolitionist, saw Cooley's case as an opportunity to introduce anti-slavery legislation.

Knowing that he did not immediately have the support for legislation, Simcoe introduced an act in 1793 to Limit Slavery in Upper Canada. It was the first piece of legislation in the British Empire to restrict enslavement.

However, full abolition was not immediately feasible—many of the province's White landowners, including members of the government, were slaveholders themselves.

The Act did not free enslaved people already in Canada, but it prohibited the importation of new slaves and declared that children born to enslaved mothers would be freed at the age of 25.

Over time, enslaved people in Upper Canada gained legal recognition, and the colony became a haven for fugitive slaves through the Underground Railroad in the 19th century.

Cooley's story is largely unknown outside of Canada although historians and African community leaders are working to change that.

Though slavery was abolished in Canada, the effects of anti-Black racism remain. African Canadians are still fighting systemic racism, economic inequality, and police violence.

Even in the aftermath of the abolition of enslavement in Upper Canada segregation in education was legally enforced as recently as the 1850s. Other acts of segregation, such as in housing still persist to this day despite legislation.

In employment African Canadian women were largely restricted to being domestic servants. Although many trade unions in Canada are now led by people of African descent, many unions during the 1950s were explicitly anti-African.

The Brotherhood of Sleeping Car Porters were the first African descendant workers to organise their own union to fight for better pay and conditions at work.

Action by campaigners of African descent and their allies forced the Canadian federal government to adopt a four-year anti-racism strategy to run from 2024–2028.

The strategy will give particular attention to addressing how anti-Black racism and the unequal treatment of Black people are entrenched and normalised in Canada.

It needs to because the situation in Canada is serious for Africans.

African descendants are over-represented in Canada's prison system, making up 9.2 per cent of the federal prison population, even though they make up only 4.3 per cent of the population.

In Canada around 41 per cent of African Canadians reported experiencing discrimination based on their race or skin colour — around 15 times higher than the proportion among the white population (3 per cent).

African men and women earn less than their white counterparts. The earnings gap is most pronounced among Canadian-origin African men, at — $16,300 (around £8,800), and least among African-origin Black men, at — $8,500 (around £4,500).

Similarly, Canadian-origin African women earn — $9,500 less (£5,126), and Caribbean-origin African women — $1,300 (£701) less compared to their white counterparts of the same generation.

As we can see Canada is not the idyllic land that many would have us believe — at least not for people of African descent.

High levels of poverty exist amongst Africans in Canada. The poverty rate in 2021 ran at around 11 per cent — almost double the rate of white folks (6 per cent).

The story of Africans in Canada is strikingly similar to the story of Africans across the diaspora.

Looking Ahead

Millions of Africans across the diaspora are sick and tired of being sick and tired.

They are fed up — as I am — of continually having to justify our very existence to people who are more than happy to have us do the dirty jobs that they don't want to do but would rather not have any of us in plain sight.

If this wasn't bad enough when we do make it into decent jobs or positions of power — even in the labour and trade union movement — we are treated as if we are interlopers.

The belief that if the role can be done by these Africans then it must be easy is, I would suggest from personal experience, not far from the mark.

Having said this, there are some reasons to be optimistic and, indeed, to be just a little bit cheerful.

Those of us in the belly of the beast who work as dissidents against the behaviours of the colonialists also have much to organise in support of the resistance and fightback by Africans.

Organisations such as the Brics bloc — Brazil, Russia, India, China and South Africa — now joined by Egypt, Ethiopia, Indonesia, Iran and the United Arab Emirates, will play an important part in building confidence amongst the diaspora to break free from US hegemony.

But, I must admit to wondering why Brics has no membership from Caribbean nations within its ranks.

Certainly Cuba took part in the South African Brics summit last year but that was through its role as president of the Group of 77 plus China bloc of nations. Certainly an important bloc representing two-thirds of the member nations of the UN and 80 per cent of the world's population.

It was an important step and the first time that Cuba has taken part in Brics and it makes sense for them, on a number of levels, for them to become a member in due course.

The fact remains, there are no Caribbean members of Brics. But what the islands of the Caribbean could bring to the table economically or politically that would make them worthwhile Brics members.

The nations of the Caribbean were once considered rich pickings for the slavers and the colonialists.

The sugar and tobacco plantations laboured by enslaved and then colonised Africans, such as my ancestors, put the equivalent of billions of pounds, dollars, francs, pesetas and gilders into the coffers of the colonial rulers.

A number of nations in the Caribbean are rich in natural resources that still help to build the economies of the rich nations, while doing seemingly little for their own as the local working and peasant classes continue to struggle to get by.

Trinidad and Tobago has vast natural gas and oil reserves even though a recent survey showed nearly a quarter of the population, 22 per cent, are regarded as poor.

Guyana, where a major oil field has recently been discovered, has around three-quarters of its population in rural areas. Around 37 of them are not just poor but live in poverty.

It seems unlikely that the poor in Guyana will get access to any of the wealth generated from the new oil fields without a fundamental shift in society in the country and a breakaway from the orbit of the major transnational oil companies, mainly from the United States, who are likely to come in, clean up and then get out.

Bauxite, essential for the manufacture of aluminium goods, is a major product of Jamaica and vital for the economies of developed countries.

The island has always had high poverty rates which, according to official statistics, now stand at around a quarter of the entire population with many people still lacking access to decent housing and clean running water.

Jamaica, as I mentioned above, relies almost entirely on tourism. Overall the industry accounts for around 70 per cent of the country's Gross Domestic Product.

Even then Jamaica, like the other Caribbean nations heavily reliant on tourism, looks for substantial foreign investment from China and the US in particular, to support the development of the industry.

Having the wealth of these Caribbean nations stripped away by the use of free or cheap labour for the benefit of the colonialists sounds awfully familiar to what happened in Africa and was explained more than 50 years ago by Walter Rodney in the brilliant book any anti-colonialist should read called *How Europe Underdeveloped Africa*.

In recent times we have seen the reaction in West and Central Africa to this continued colonial process and I predict that we will soon see the same reaction by the poor nations of the Caribbean.

Leaving the Caribbean as a holiday playground after the colonialists stripped bare their natural resources is not the basis for being invited to sit at the big kids' table.

It is also not something that the working class and peasant communities of those countries will continue to put up with.

The Caribbean is effectively still under the iron heel of colonialism.

It can be given a pretty new name of the Commonwealth — as if the wealth coming from the nations was going to be shared — but it is still colonialism in any way it is shaken.

Many of these countries, such as Jamaica, St Lucia, Trinidad and Tobago, and The Bahamas, are theoretically independent island nations within the Commonwealth.

Barbados became an independent republic within the Commonwealth in 2021.

This still leaves them all too close to the British as the former colonial power. Indeed the final court of appeal for each of these countries is still in Britain.

How can you be independent if you can't have the final say over your laws?

It's a similar tale for French Caribbean nations, such as Guadeloupe, Martinique as well as Dutch Suriname.

The French Caribbean islands are all official departments of France so there is only the pretence of independence when a small group of people sitting in plush surroundings thousands of miles away even get to decide on the proper use of French in your country.

Suriname is independent but also has a close relationship with its former colonial master the Netherlands.

It simply would not make much sense to allow the influence that the colonists could bring to bear over these 'not really yet independent' nations inside of Brics.

Brics is about creating new rules of the game. By definition this means not allowing the old bullying tactics that the colonialists adopt to seep into the work of Brics.

But, beyond Brics, the question for the nations of the Caribbean is how and when they will fully break the ties with their former colonial rulers.

I believe that the working class and peasant communities struggling to survive in the Caribbean will be looking across the sacred burial grounds of the Atlantic Ocean and watching their ancestors rise up against the plundering of the wealth of their countries by the colonialists.

They will see the similarities and will soon come to the conclusion that those politicians acting as clients for the generation of even more wealth for the colonialists, while they wonder where the next meal will come from, should be swept aside and replaced with people who represent their class interests.

Reggae legend Peter Tosh once said:

'Hungry people are angry people.'

Don't be surprised if we soon see that anger turn into action across the Caribbean.

'A united family eats from the same plate.'

— *African proverb*

CHAPTER TEN — REFLECTIONS

IN A PARAPHRASE of the writer Henry James, it's a complex fate to be African.

We exist or, perhaps more accurately, survive in the belly of the beast called Babylon. The beast that uprooted us by force, sold us with less care than they would the cheapest food and then treated us worse than any animal.

Once the model for making huge, unimaginable profits, called the transatlantic slave trade, was made unworkable by the rebellion of the enslaved they then colonised us to maintain control of the natural resources needed to maintain the enriched lifestyle that their people had come to expect.

The 'they' I refer to isn't some mysterious individual. It is the big business interests that were behind the trade. The organisations that made the seriously big money — and are still doing so.

Living in the belly of Babylon gives us a very particular view of life.

It is a view based on the knowledge that we are not really wanted. They often only really want us here to fill in the gaps that the poor white working class cannot or don't want to fill, to clean toilets, sweep floors and do the other 'undesired' jobs which require an early start and a late finish after your second or third job.

When we are no longer needed, as the economy tightens, we get treated like the 'unpeople', the commodities we have become, and discarded usually with the consent manufactured by a wave of racism.

For the little we are given we are supposed to be eternally grateful and told that if we don't like it we should go back 'home' or 'go back to where you came from.'

Being born and brought up in Walsall in the heart of the Black Country I always found this a really weird insult from the racists who have far too regularly dogged my life.

Even when they don't make these insults directly to us I have always found it fairly amusing that they don't think Black people have learnt to read the body language or tone of comments to know racism as well as we do the back of our own hands.

I don't pretend to speak on behalf of all Black people, although those of us who have been involved in some of the spaces that I have occupied are often expected to do so.

But I know from private conversations and the glances I often receive from other Black people that they too can read the real meaning behind the words or actions just as well as I can.

That's why it's important that we think carefully when organising conferences on the situation facing the working class or peasant communities across the globe.

We people of 'the darker nations' or the Third World or Global South, depending on your preference, tend to come at things from an angle that may be nuanced, even as Marxists, from other comrades who do not share our heritage.

I raise this simple point to illustrate the importance of providing space for this experience in our development of strategies to help us create a new world.

Any group or conference on internationalism needs to understand that millions of us from the Third World or Global South live in the belly of the vicious and exploitative Global North beast. Our experience is unique and important.

We hold a different perspective that encompasses our experiences from where we physically stay as well as our emotional attachment to our ancestral homes.

The task for this and every socialist-oriented international gathering is to work out the best way of doing more than merely taking this experience into account in a theoretical sense, but also how to use this to build the movement that will be necessary to help birth the new world.

I think there are a number of key questions that all of us, whatever our backgrounds need to ask.

Does the rise of Africa alter the balance of power in favour of the working class within the North? Will the rise of Africa help to bring peace to the world? Will the creation of a multilateral world do anything to alleviate the deep-seated institutional inequality across the globe? Will the climate emergency be tackled?

The answer to each of these questions is probably not unless we organise to break the back of the beast from within.

We must ask whether the rampant racism that has blighted the lives of Africans will be tackled? Will the fact that Africa is already being destroyed by climate change be a high enough priority for world leaders?

In my experience, things change because working-class and peasant peoples across the globe make them change and never, as far as I can see, because of the largesse of some benevolent politician.

It seems to me that organising alongside sound political theory is always the key to progress.

But part of that formula must include an understanding or, at the very least, a space for the particular heritage and experiences that come from being African while being born and bred in the North.

The Importance of Walter Rodney

One of the joys of writing this book has been the prompt to re-read some of the classic texts on African liberation.

One of these texts was written by someone who has always been inspirational in helping to shape my political outlook — the great Guyanese scholar and activist Walter Rodney.

His classic 1972 book *How Europe Underdeveloped Africa* is, in my view, one of the seminal texts that must be read by anyone who is serious about understanding why Africa is in the shape that it is.

It also provides a Marxist and Pan-Africanist framework for helping to build an understanding of how the continent can break away from the endemic humiliation and exploitation it has faced for 500 years.

The book helps to provide clarity as to why there can be economic progress in some African nations whilst millions of Africans live in the most abject poverty with lower life expectancy, sky-high levels of unemployment with the informal sector far outstripping the security of formal employment and the benefits of trade unionism.

Rodney was an academic as well as a working-class revolutionary who was heavily influenced by Marxism.

But Rodney was never afraid to use the tool that Marxism provides to develop new thinking that took account of the material circumstances facing the working class and peasant populations of the Global South.

Rodney was able to bring together several traditions that engaged with the Global South experience.

As well as having a deep understanding of Marxism, Rodney was able to engage confidently with the thoughts of Martinique's Frantz Fanon, the Pan-Africanist tradition of the likes of George Padmore and C.L.R. James as well as the ideas of African socialism put forward by Tanzania's Julius Nyerere and Guinea's Ahmed Sékou Touré.

Being open to this range of ideas meant that Rodney was not boxed into trying to explain the material circumstances that faced the Global South by simply trying to equate them with Europe and applying what might work there to working-class and peasant communities on the African continent.

Rodney, along with C.L.R. James, was one of the first people who was ever able to explain to me the legacies of enslavement, colonialism and underdevelopment in a way that you didn't have to swallow a Marxist dictionary to be able to understand.

I realise that to some this might be heretical to some reading this where the mastery of theory is turned into a weapon to be used against people that don't quite meet the standards.

I'm not against theory in the slightest — it is vital to have a firm grasp of Marxist theory — as I have said in these pages before.

But unless we are able to understand how this theory can be turned into revolutionary action then it is not much more than arrogant self-indulgence.

Rodney believed that Africa — far from standing outside the world system — has been absolutely central to the growth of Western capitalism.

According to Rodney, this growth was only achieved by the underdevelopment of the African continent through centuries of enslavement, exploitation and imperialism.

Rodney shows that Europe did not merely enrich their own empires but deliberately blocked economic and social development in Africa.

By utilising his immense skills as a historian Rodney was able to demonstrate how the West was built on the backs of Africans and through the ruthless extraction of the continent's natural resources.

He talks about how the underdevelopment of Africa is historically produced through capitalist expansion and imperialism. It creates value and wealth for the Western ruling class while making the exploited poorer.

The so-called trading relationship between Europe and Africa was in fact no trade at all. It was pure exploitation.

This exploitation was integral to the unequal relationship that was closely tied up with the growth of European port cities such as Liverpool, with the exchange of enslaved Africans for cheap industrial goods.

The bottom line was that the trade in African human beings provided the British with the capital that was necessary for the success of the Industrial Revolution.

The vastly unequal trade relations meant that technological development across the continent stagnated and blocked the means by which innovation could take place.

As I illustrated earlier in this book the so-called 'scramble for Africa' led to the exploitation of the vast wealth of raw materials of the continent. Something that we are still witnessing today.

I also pointed out how racism was used to justify European imperialism and how this has always been met by resistance by Africans — whether on the African continent or across the diaspora.

But, as Rodney makes clear in his writings, it is an inescapable fact that the colonisation of Africa was an 'indispensable link in a chain of events which made possible the technological transformation of the base of European capitalism.'

Uranium, copper and cobalt from the Congo, iron from West Africa, chrome from Rhodesia and South Africa were vital for the development of Western capitalism.

Rodney was able to point all of this out in the early 1970s as well as organise in Guyana to develop a Marxist and Pan-Africanist response.

This was scary to the establishment and led to him being killed by the social democrat forces in the country.

This book has leant heavily on the thoughts of Rodney and many other leading Marxist writers of African descent to help to set out some of the challenges — often competing — that face Africans on the continent and across the diaspora in organising for and building a new multilateral world.

My contention is that Africa will play one of the leading roles in that new multilateral world.

Africa and Africans wherever we are will do so by standing on the shoulders of giants such as Rodney and understanding that we don't need to wait for a hero to emerge to guide us.

We can rebirth Africa through a belief in our own collective strength and understanding that many others, such as Rodney, have already provided us with much of the theoretical foundations we need.

Our job is to add to those foundations where we need to and build on them solid structures based on the principles of Marxism and Pan-Africanism.

The Defining Story of the 21st Century

The rise of the continent of Africa and its peoples worldwide will be the defining story of the remaining decades of the 21st century. Each chapter of this book provides an understanding of how this might be achieved.

According to every reputable survey the population of the continent will reach around 2.5 billion by the midpoint of this century. This means that it will account for around a quarter of the world's population.

Most studies also show that sub-Saharan Africa will soon become the only place on the planet with rising birth rates, whilst most major economies, such as the US, China and the entirety of Europe are likely to see a drop.

The median age for the continent is 18, 14 years younger than any other region.

The demographics for the vast African continent are astonishing but we are likely to see — unless action is taken — a widening gap between the rich and the poor.

Africa boasts 30 per cent of the world's mineral reserves which will make it a continued target for extraction by the Western powers or will help to pull the continent out of the underdevelopment primarily caused by the Europeans.

The Congo alone holds over 70 per cent of the world's cobalt, a highly versatile metal with numerous commercial applications and a critical input for the production of lithium-ion batteries for electric vehicles.

Leveraging this demand to generate revenues that can be used for financing developmental goals will be crucial if African nations are to achieve economic stability and growth and with it a genuine independence.

Much of the exploitation of the continent has been enabled by the corruption of vassals who have been prepared for many decades to do the bidding of the colonial powers.

If we understand this then we begin to understand what has happened in recent years in Niger, Mali, Burkina Faso and other places in Western Africa.

These nations have risen up against these Western client regimes and removed them from power in a bid to reclaim the vast resources in these countries for the use of the people.

The research for this book and the uprising across West Africa against the former colonial ruler France have also prompted me to re-read *The Wretched of the Earth* by the brilliant Frantz Fanon.

Fanon makes the case for the right of colonised peoples to fight for their freedom by, in the words of Malcolm X, 'any means necessary', including violence.

This right, Fanon argues, is based on the notion that as colonisers generally consider the colonised to be subhuman they should not be bound by principles that apply to humanity in the way that they conduct their fight against the coloniser.

For Fanon, violent resistance to colonialism is inevitable as the presence of the coloniser is largely based on military strength. In fact, more than an inevitability, violence is something of a necessity imposed on the colonised by the colonisers.

As a descendent of colonised and, before that, enslaved people, I have every sympathy with people who live under the boot of oppression using force to remove the iron heel of their oppressor.

A glance through examples of colonial rule provides enough evidence of the vicious use of violence to enforce colonialism and the unfortunate need of the colonised to use force to resist their oppression and win their freedom.

The resistance to the illegal Israeli occupation of the West Bank and their treatment of the Palestinians provides an obvious example.

I do not point the use of violence out with any glee. Far from it. But I have not been able to find a single instance where any country colonising another land has voluntarily given up that land out of the goodness of their heart.

Factors external to the colonised land, such as domestic troubles in the land of the colonisers or occupying forces being needed to quell attacks against their interests elsewhere are amongst the reasons they might leave.

Usually, as far as I can see, colonisers leave because the colonised no longer cooperate with them and have made their lands ungovernable.

Given the response to non-cooperation to colonial rule is always, without exception, violent, that seems to me to leave oppressed people with little choice but to either take the violent response or resist it.

So, in many respects, the only surprising things about events in Niger are that it didn't happen sooner and that it is not more widespread given the way that colonial powers such as France still continue to profit off the backs of people in Niger.

Many people in Niger live in the sort of gut-wrenching poverty that many in the Global North can only ever imagine. But they know their country possesses vast resources of gold and uranium that make the Global North, particularly their former colonial ruler France, both rich and powerful.

They also realise that 'Fortress Europe' bars them from moving northwards to get a slice of the wealth that they helped to produce.

They see their country being talked of as an important strategic place where space-age drone stations are built from which attacks can be launched against anyone seen as an opponent of an empire many thousands of miles away — but not necessarily a foe of theirs.

They can easily see themselves being used as a pawn in someone else's global game of dominance. But mostly they see themselves struggling to survive while others just get richer and more powerful off their backs.

France, in common with other European states, depends heavily on the uranium produced in Niger to fuel its domestic electricity supply.

Around a third of France's electricity supply depends on uranium.

While the famous Eiffel Tower in Paris and many parts of France can afford to keep their lights on for show or even for security purposes, just 18 per cent of Nigeriens have access to the electricity that their hard labour has produced.

Niger is the world's fifth-largest uranium producer.

Figures in 2021 showed that Niger provided nearly a quarter of the European Union's uranium supplies.

The French nuclear company, formerly, Areva and now Orano — began mining in Niger in the 1970s.

In 2021 one of the four pits, in the northern town of Arlit, closed down leaving thousands unemployed and the local population having to live next to around 20 million tonnes of radioactive mud on the site.

The local soil and underground water tables have been found to be severely contaminated but the local population of around 100,000 have little alternative but to continue drinking the polluted water leading to cancer and birth defects amongst other things.

It escapes me why anyone would think this sort of treatment in Niger, or the exploitation of people for cobalt, gold, diamonds and so much more in Africa will go unchallenged.

People always eventually rise up against exploitation and this is essentially what we are saying across parts of Western Africa — the land of my ancestors.

The colonisers are still exploiting Africa. But they need to remove themselves and allow any problems, within these artificial borders created by them, to be dealt with by the people of the continent themselves.

If they refuse to remove themselves voluntarily then Africans must rise up on the continent and across the diaspora to remove them as well as the charlatans that do their bidding on the motherland.

The great lesson of this book is for Africans, wherever we are, to understand that resistance to racism and all forms of exploitation is in our DNA. We have survived hundreds of years of exploitation because we have understood the strength that comes from building communities of resistance.

Those that dominated us never thought we had the capacity to survive so now fear us as we stand on the threshold of exercising our independence of body and mind.

They are right to fear us! We are strong and we will win!

How will we win?

I have attempted to show in this book that resistance will only come through a unity of will and purpose.

That is how Africans have managed to survive against all the odds for so long.

But we cannot succeed on our own. Africans must — build our own solidarity on the continent itself or wherever we find ourselves. But it is vital that we build communities of resistance with working class and peasant communities who are white, Asian or indigenous.

There are many organisations across the globe that are campaigning around issues relating to each of the separate chapters in this book. If we are to see the rebirth of Africa then we must unite these struggles under the common aim of building a worldwide movement for socialism.

That means that Africans must make a common bond with others across the globe who share our aims. A colour or narrow nationalistic approach will not be sufficient to succeed. In fact this would be our undoing.

The rebirth of Africa will only actually take place if we recognise that not only are we interdependent with each other as Africans but that we are also dependent on each other as working class and peasants across the globe.

We simply cannot rely on anyone else to intervene on our behalf or to do the work for us.

So my call is for a new and refreshed Communist International type body to support the process of African rebirth.

The Communist International (Comintern) was an international organisation that united the communist parties of different countries between 1919 and 1943.

Founded by the great Vladimir Lenin, its aim was to spread the ideas of revolutionary socialism. The clash between these two organisations occurred due to different approaches to World War I and the October Revolution in Russia.

Moscow hosted the First Comintern Congress on March 2–6, 1919.

Fifty-two delegates from 34 parties across the globe attended the Congress. They decided to create an Executive Committee composed of representatives from the most significant communist groups and parties.

Grigory Zinoviev was appointed as the Chairman of the Executive Committee to manage the work of the Comintern.

Lenin was the key driving force behind the Comintern until his death in January 1924.

The main objective of the Comintern was to establish communist parties worldwide to support the worldwide revolution of the working class.

The parties also adhered to his democratic centralism philosophy, which stated that communist parties should make decisions democratically and adhere to those decisions in a disciplined manner.

I am not convinced by the need or practicality of a body to oversee the work of rebirthing Africa and the worldwide revolution but I am more convinced than ever that socialism is the way forward for the people of Africa on the continent and across the diaspora.

I am also convinced that some coordination of this rebirth is essential.

I think this can only succeed if we adopt the principles that have become the cornerstone of the Brics bloc mentioned earlier in this book.

At its core the Brics looks to foster close working relations between member nations — mainly on trade and technology — alongside a firm commitment for non-interference in the internal affairs of each country.

Whatever the organisation looks it must take its guidance from the material circumstances that exist on the ground and not try to shoehorn any particular approach that may have worked — or not worked — from elsewhere.

We can draw on the great work being done by organisations such as the Tricontinental Institute for Social Research under the inspirational leadership of Indian Marxist Vijay Prashad.

The Tricontinental produces a groundbreaking analysis of the challenges facing the Global South and can be relied on to draw the parallels that exist between the material circumstances facing Africans and others across the globe.

We can also make better collective use of those people-focused media such as the US-based Breakthrough News and Black Agenda Report. But all of this requires coordination rather than what seems at times to be a rather haphazard approach to liberation.

The choice we face is to carry on doing the same things that we have always done whilst expecting different results or a radical new approach that rises above the sometimes sectarian or superior approaches that have sometimes dogged our movement for socialism.

I favour doing something new to support the rebirth of the mother continent and all those who are descended from it across the globe.

From my perch in Babylon I see the potential for real and fundamental change in favour of working class and peasant communities across the globe with Africa and Africans at its heart.

In fact it is more than potential. It is also more than necessary. It has already begun. Our job now is to be the midwives of that birth.

The waters have broken. The head has appeared. Africa is about to be reborn.

'People get Ready, there's a train comin'
You don't need no baggage, you just get on board
All you need is faith, to hear the diesels hummin'
Don't need no ticket, you just thank the Lord.'

— *Curtis Mayfield*